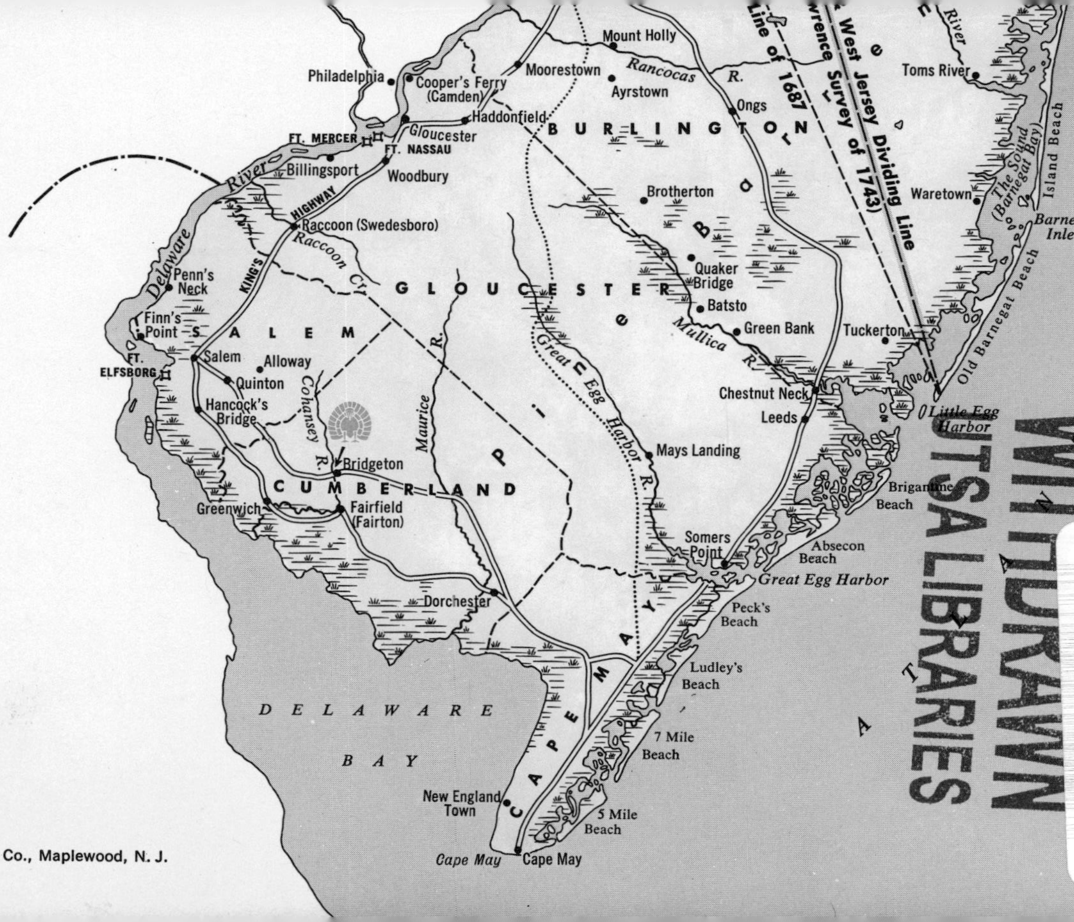

Philadelphia
Cooper's Ferry (Camden)
Moorestown
Mount Holly
Rancocas R.
Ayrstown
Haddonfield
Ongs
BURLINGTON
Gloucester
FT. MERCER
FT. NASSAU
Billingsport
Woodbury
Delaware River
KING'S HIGHWAY
Raccoon (Swedesboro)
Raccoon Cr.
Brotherton
Quaker Bridge
Batsto
Green Bank
Mullica R.
GLOUCESTER
Penn's Neck
Finn's Point
SALEM
FT. ELFSBORG
Salem
Alloway
Quinton
Hancock's Bridge
Cohansey R.
Maurice R.
Great Egg Harbor R.
Bridgeton
CUMBERLAND
Greenwich
Fairfield (Fairton)
Mays Landing
Chestnut Neck
Leeds
Tuckerton
Somers Point
Dorchester
CAPE MAY
DELAWARE BAY
New England Town
Cape May
Cape May
Line of 1687
West Jersey Dividing Line
Survey of 1743)
Toms River
River
Waretown
The Sound (Barnegat Bay)
Island Beach
Barnegat Inlet
Old Barnegat Beach
Little Egg Harbor
Brigantine Beach
Absecon Beach
Great Egg Harbor
Peck's Beach
Ludley's Beach
7 Mile Beach
5 Mile Beach
ATLANTIC OCEAN

Princeton and Rutgers

THE NEW JERSEY HISTORICAL SERIES

Edited by

RICHARD M. HUBER   WHEATON J. LANE

New Jersey from Colony to State—1609-1789	Richard P. McCormick
New Jersey and the Civil War	Earl Schenck Miers
New Jersey and the English Colonization of North America	Wesley Frank Craven
The Story of the Jersey Shore	Harold F. Wilson
Princeton and Rutgers—Two Colonial Colleges in New Jersey	George P. Schmidt
Architecture in New Jersey	Alan Gowans
Elementary Education in New Jersey—A History	Roscoe L. West
The New Jersey High School—A History	Robert D. Bole and Laurence B. Johnson
The New Jersey Proprietors and Their Lands	John E. Pomfret
The Early Dutch and Swedish Settlers of New Jersey	Adrian C. Leiby
New Jersey and the American Revolution	Alfred Hoyt Bill

Other books in the series will be announced

Volume 5
The New Jersey Historical Series

Princeton and Rutgers

THE TWO COLONIAL COLLEGES OF NEW JERSEY

GEORGE P. SCHMIDT

1964

D. VAN NOSTRAND COMPANY, INC.
Princeton, New Jersey
New York, N. Y. • Toronto, Canada • London, England

D. VAN NOSTRAND COMPANY, INC.
120 Alexander St., Princeton, New Jersey (*Principal office*)
24 West 40 Street, New York 18, New York

D. VAN NOSTRAND COMPANY, LTD.
358, Kensington High Street, London, W.14, England

D. VAN NOSTRAND COMPANY (*Canada*), LTD.
25 Hollinger Road, Toronto 16, Canada

Published simultaneously in Canada by
D. VAN NOSTRAND COMPANY (Canada), LTD.

PRINTED IN THE UNITED STATES OF AMERICA

FOREWORD

Many tracks will be left by the New Jersey Tercentenary celebration, but few will be larger than those made by the New Jersey Historical Series. The Series is a monumental publishing project—the product of a remarkable collaborative effort between public and private enterprise.

New Jersey has needed a series of books about itself. The 300th anniversary of the State is a fitting time to publish such a series. It is to the credit of the State's Tercentenary Commission that this series has been created.

In an enterprise of such scope, there must be many contributors. Each of these must give considerably of himself if the enterprise is to succeed. The New Jersey Historical Series, the most ambitious publishing venture ever undertaken about a state, was conceived by a committee of Jerseymen—Julian F. Boyd, Wesley Frank Craven, John T. Cunningham, David S. Davies, and Richard P. McCormick. Not only did these men outline the need for such an historic venture; they also aided in the selection of the editors of the series.

Both jobs were well done. The volumes speak for themselves. The devoted and scholarly services of

Richard M. Huber and Wheaton J. Lane, the editors, are a part of every book in the series. The editors have been aided in their work by two fine assistants, Elizabeth Jackson Holland and Bertha DeGraw Miller.

To D. Van Nostrand Company, Inc. my special thanks for recognizing New Jersey's need and for bringing their skills and publishing wisdom to bear upon the printing and distributing of the New Jersey Historical Series.

RICHARD J. HUGHES
Governor of the State of New Jersey

January, 1964

PREFACE

It need hardly be pointed out that this little volume is not intended as a full-length history of either Princeton or Rutgers. Such extended treatment is obviously impossible within the scope of the book; besides, that is not the purpose. The purpose is to portray those significant events in the history of the two institutions that illustrate their relations to the State of New Jersey and to each other. Everything else has had to be eliminated or rigorously compressed. Accordingly, I have selected that which I thought most important and have presented it against the background of the history of New Jersey and of American higher education in general. Much interesting material has been left out. Thus, I have been able to mention only a few of the hundreds of alumni of both institutions who had prominent careers in New Jersey and rendered signal service to the state.

Various people have helped me in this undertaking. I am particularly indebted to Donald A. Sinclair, Curator of Special Collections in the Rutgers University Library, and to M. Halsey Thomas, Archivist of Princeton University, for their courtesy and their help in making their collections available to me. Roger H. McDonough, Director of the State Library in Trenton, called my attention to various sources and provided some of them for my use. The Editors of the Tercentenary Series, Richard M. Huber and Wheaton J. Lane, have encouraged me at all times and made many helpful suggestions. Finally, I am grateful to the two editorial assistants, Mrs. Elizabeth

A. Holland originally, and latterly Mrs. Bertha D. Miller, for smoothing the way and keeping communications open. Mrs. Miller has prepared the Appendix of the degree granting colleges and universities in New Jersey, and has also secured the illustrations from the archives of the two universities.

New Brunswick, N. J.
February, 1964

George P. Schmidt

CONTENTS

LIST OF ILLUSTRATIONS

I

COLONIAL BEGINNINGS

ON THE EVE of the American Revolution nine little colleges lay scattered over the mainland of British North America. The four New England colonies had one each, of which Harvard, founded in 1636, was the first. There was one in New York, one in Pennsylvania, one in Virginia. New Jersey had two such colleges: Princeton, chartered as the College of New Jersey in 1746, and Rutgers, chartered as Queen's College in 1766. They were the fourth and the eighth in order of founding.

The presence of two institutions of higher learning in such a small colony did not mean that Jerseymen were intellectually superior to their fellow-Americans. In fact, Jonathan Belcher may have come closer to appraising the true state of affairs when, on assuming the governorship of the province in 1747, he characterized his new subjects as "a very rustical people, and deficient in learning." * The dual experiment in higher education was rather the result of the religious, national, and social stratification of this middle colony, trying to maintain its identity between its two large neighbors, New York and Pennsylvania, and receiving the overflow population of both. A royal province since 1702, when the East and West Jersey proprietorships were merged, New Jersey shared its chief executive with New York until 1735. Even after it had its own governor and achieved status

* Allan Nevins, *The American States During and After the Revolution* (New York, 1927), 44.

as a completely separate province, its earlier split personality was not completely fused, for the legislature was required to meet in Amboy and Burlington alternately.

The population, approaching one hundred thousand by the middle of the eighteenth century, was mixed. The first settlers to come in any number were Dutch farmers who crossed the Hudson from New Amsterdam, pushed up the valleys of the Hackensack, the Passaic, and the Raritan, and established their culture in these northern and central regions. Among them were numerous Walloons and French Huguenots. Rutgers owes its beginning to these people. English stock came from New England and New York and settled Newark, Elizabeth, and surrounding areas. At the other end of the province, English Quakers mingled with the descendants of earlier Swedish settlers. Religious affiliations of the English population were Anglican or Puritan or Quaker. The Swedes, originally Lutheran, were largely absorbed into the Anglican group. In the second quarter of the eighteenth century immigrants from Scotland and Ulster came in great numbers, entering through the ports of New York or Amboy or Philadelphia. They brought the Presbyterian faith with them, and they launched the college in Princeton. In addition to all these, there were German Lutheran and Moravian communities and minor groups.

This milling mass of ex-Europeans in process of becoming Americans was further stirred, in the third decade of the century, by a religious and emotional upheaval known in American history as the Great Awakening. Leaving none of the denominational and national groups untouched, the revival had its greatest effect upon the Dutch Reformed and the Scottish Presbyterian churches, where it unleashed forces and set in motion a train of events that culminated in the establishment of two institutions of higher learning. Leaders in the revival were the Reverend Theodorus Jacobus Frelinghuysen, American founder of the family which has continued prominent in New Jersey history from that day to this, and the brothers Gilbert and William Tennent, Presbyterian ministers.

A native of the Netherlands, Frelinghuysen came to New Jersey in 1720 with a degree from the University of Halle in Germany. Halle was at that time the center of a strong pietistic and evangelical movement in European Protestantism, a movement which emphasized the emotional and ethical elements in Christianity while minimizing doctrine and ritual. The Tennent brothers had studied the classics and theology at a primitive but scholastically sound "log college" which their father, also a minister, conducted in his parish at Neshaminy, Pennsylvania. Frelinghuysen and the Tennents met in the Raritan valley, where all held pastorates. Holding similar convictions on the importance of personal experience and religious dedication as opposed to formal orthodoxy, they joined forces to promote an evangelical revival which soon swept through the churches like a brush fire, leaping over denominational barriers. In their excess of zeal, the enthusiasts antagonized the conservative elements in both denominations, who resented being called lax and indifferent. There was understandable indignation when Gilbert Tennent denounced those ministers who failed to share his views or approve his methods as "dead dogs, madmen, and enemies of God." * The result was a split in both the Scottish and the Dutch churches along conservative-progressive lines. Deprived of a continuing source of preachers for their expanding activities by conservative control of the denominational administrative machinery, the progressives came to the conclusion that they would have to establish their own educational institutions. For with all their emphasis on emotion and spirituality, they remained firm believers in an educated ministry.

The Presbyterians, with greater numbers and wider associations than the Reformed churches, moved first. They were joined at this point by several preachers from

* Thomas J. Wertenbaker, *Princeton 1746-1896* (Princeton, 1946), 8.

New England, graduates of Yale, who had taken parishes in New Jersey and were in full accord with the evangelical faction. In fact, the New England pastors spearheaded the movement. It was Yale's Jonathan Dickinson and Aaron Burr who appointed themselves trustees, along with two other preachers and three laymen, and secured a charter in 1746 for a collegiate institution that was to be known as "The College of New Jersey." The Tennents and the rest of the Scotch-Irish group were then brought into membership when the trustees were increased to 23 in the second, revised charter of 1748. Meanwhile, classes had opened in May, 1747, when ten young men met in Elizabeth in the home of Dickinson, who had been chosen the first president. Dickinson had hardly taken office when he died and was succeeded by Aaron Burr. In Burr's Newark parsonage the work of the College was carried on for the next eight years. But Newark was too far from the main Presbyterian communities to be acceptable as a permanent location. Peace offerings were being made to the conservative wing, whose strength was concentrated in and around Philadelphia, and it seemed desirable to move closer to that center. For a while, New Brunswick was favorably considered, and the College would have settled there had the town met the trustees' requirements of a thousand pounds in New Jersey currency plus ten acres for a campus and two hundred acres of woodland for fuel. But New Brunswick failed at the last moment to raise the full amount; the village of Princeton meanwhile met all the conditions, and the College was permanently established there. On the main stage road from New York to Philadelphia, Princeton was as readily accessible as New Brunswick; and besides, in the opinion of Princeton's historian, "it was well protected from the once famous New Jersey mosquito." *

The next step was a college building. Designed by Robert Smith of Philadelphia, who had also drawn

* Thomas J. Wertenbaker, *Princeton 1746-1896* (Princeton, 1946), 37.

the plans for Carpenters' Hall and other buildings in that city, the 177-foot, four-story structure was the largest in British North America. At the suggestion of Governor Belcher it was named Nassau Hall, in memory of King William III of the House of Orange and Nassau, liberal English monarch and friend of Dissenters. With funds collected on two continents the building was completed in 1756; in November of that year President Burr brought his 70 students and three tutors down from Newark, and the College of New Jersey moved into Nassau Hall. Few American colleges have been identified so completely, and for so long a time, with their first building. For over a hundred years the name of the building was used, informally, as a designation for the college; the formal name, The College of New Jersey, seems never to have been very popular.

Twenty years after the Presbyterians had established their college, the evangelical leaders among the Dutch Reformed churches obtained authorization for a college of their own. In order to secure it, they had virtually to declare their independence from the source of ecclesiastical authority of the Dutch church, the Classis of Amsterdam, which did not favor the enterprise and barred its supporters from soliciting funds in the mother country. There was initial opposition, too, from the conservative wing of the Dutch churches in America, and this had to be overcome gradually. Unlike their Presbyterian brethren, who could count on support from members of their own household of faith throughout the colonies, the Dutch were concentrated in New York and New Jersey, and even there they were under constant pressure to merge with their English and Scottish neighbors and fellow-subjects of the British Crown. It was therefore quite an achievement when, in November, 1766, they finally secured a charter, emanating from King George III, through the instrumentality of Royal Governor William Franklin, and authorizing them to establish an institution of higher learning to be known as Queen's College.

Now there was a charter, but that was all. For the next five years little happened. There were no students, no professors, no buildings, nothing but a series of trustees' meetings. The Classis of Amsterdam, still influential, pressed for union with the College of New Jersey at Princeton, while some of the New York City brethren suggested a merger with the newly established (1754) King's College in that city. Neither suggestion was accepted; instead, the sponsors secured a second, confirming, charter in 1770, and the enterprise was now able to get under way. No copy of the original Charter of 1766 is known to exist. The very fact that there was one passed from men's memory for over a hundred years. When the Centennial of Rutgers was to be celebrated, the year mistakenly chosen for the event was 1870.

Two New Jersey towns vied for the location of the college: New Brunswick once again, and Hackensack. This time New Brunswick was forward. Not willing to lose a second time, it offered a larger financial inducement and was chosen over Hackensack by the trustees by a vote of ten to seven. In November, 1771, five years after the granting of the first charter, classes opened in a house at the corner of what is now Albany and Neilson Streets, under a tutor, Frederick Frelinghuysen, grandson of Theodorus Frelinghuysen who had started the whole movement. The younger Frelinghuysen was eighteen years old and a graduate of the College of New Jersey, class of 1770. The number of entering students that year is not known, but the first graduating class, in 1774, consisted of one man, Matthew Leydt. He had the commencement program all to himself, delivering orations in Latin, Dutch, and English "with high applause." * The second graduating class had five members.

New Jersey, then, had two functioning colleges before the War for Independence. The older one in Princeton was much the larger. A hundred and twenty under-

* William H. S. Demarest, *A History of Rutgers College 1766-1924* (New Brunswick, 1924), 90.

graduates were quartered in Nassau Hall by 1770, though the number fell off sharply during the Revolution and for some years thereafter. Queen's, with a later start and a smaller constituency, had a more tenuous existence and enrolled few students before the war. Neither institution would have survived had it not been for the ability, devotion, and almost superhuman exertions of the officers in charge. Four of the first five presidents of the College of New Jersey may be said, with little exaggeration, to have killed themselves in office. Aaron Burr continued to serve his Newark congregation while doing nearly all the teaching and attending to all the administrative and financial chores which the presidency brought with it. When the establishment was shifted from Newark to Princeton he advanced his own money to students for moving expenses. He made many long journeys in the interest of the College in a day when traveling was a real hardship, and he did all this for three years without salary. Small wonder that his successor, Samuel Davies, timidly requested in a self-distrustful letter of acceptance that claret, beer, candles, and cheese be guaranteed as perquisites of the presidential office. Jacob R. Hardenbergh, first president of Queen's, was cast in a heroic mold. Though pastor of a busy parish, he found time to undertake the perilous journey to Holland to secure approval and support for the College, then he served as a key member of its board of trustees, as acting president during the trying war years, and finally as the first formally elected president. He died at fifty-four, worn out by his incessant efforts to ward off bankruptcy and keep the infant institution alive.

Other pioneers of religion and learning who assisted the first presidents were the Tennent brothers and the four sons of Theodorus Frelinghuysen, to mention only the most prominent. These men carried impossible burdens of work, yet found time to travel the length of the continent, accepting all the hardships of the road, in the interest of their college; some of them undertook the even greater hazards and uncertainties of a journey to Europe which meant years of separation from their families; and they died, at least by twentieth-century standards, long before their time. Of their efforts, two American universities were born.

The immediate goal of all these efforts, of both the Presbyterian and the Reformed group, was the securing of a charter which would give their educational enterprise legal existence and the right to conduct its affairs within the framework of the provincial society of the day. The charter, a familiar legal device going back in English common law to the Middle Ages and on the Continent to Roman times, had been widely used to organize not only political communities but economic groups such as merchant and craft guilds and, later, the trading corporations and stock companies so familiar to students of American colonial history. It also proved a convenient instrument for establishing institutions of learning. But, as in so many cases when European institutions crossed the ocean to the new world, significant differences soon appeared. The charters of the colleges that made up the universities of Oxford and Cambridge authorized the resident masters to administer external affairs and to choose one of their number as titular head: or, as we would say today, the faculty governed the college, without any additional organized body of rulers or administrators between it and the Crown, or the public.

But in a new country, possessing little in the way of accumulated capital endowment for the pursuit of scholarship and less reverence for its traditions, and with no national government to appeal to for its support, institutions of higher learning could not hope to maintain themselves without the active participation of responsible and influential members of the community, both lay and clerical. This became apparent when Yale was founded, nearly half a century before Princeton. Harvard and William and Mary, both of which preceded Yale, had tried to carry on in the Cambridge and Oxford manner, with the president and fellows (faculty) as the chief governing body. But the Yale charter created a board of trustees made up of colonial officials, leading clergymen, and prominent lay leaders, all of them external to the faculty. It did not take long for this form of organization to demonstrate its usefulness in the competitive, rapidly changing, and loosely governed American society. In time Yale's independent board of trustees, standing between the academic community and the public, became the pattern for most American colleges and universities. Such a board was indispensable in getting a new institution started. It was a channel of continuing financial support and the means of interpreting the layman and the scholar, town and gown, to one another.

The two New Jersey colleges were no exception to this pattern. The charters of both, as stated, were granted by the Crown, that of the College of New Jersey through Governor Jonathan Belcher, that of Queen's through Governor William Franklin. Both charters created boards of trustees which had to include, *ex officio,* the governor of the province and several other public officials. To this day the governor of New Jersey is authorized to preside, if he desires, at all meetings of the trustees of both Princeton and Rutgers, and he does preside at the inauguration of every president of each university. Apart from the *ex officio* members, both boards were to be self-perpetuating, filling their own vacancies. Though the religious motive had been dominant in the founding of each and was to continue so for years, neither institution could be called a church college in any legal sense, for neither was owned or directly governed by any organized religious body. The charter of the College of New Jersey provided for a maximum of 23 trustees of whom twelve had to be residents of New Jersey; the actual first board had five provincial officials, six laymen, and twelve Presbyterian ministers. Some of the early vacancies in the clerical contingent were filled with ministers of the Dutch Reformed church, so similar to the Presbyterian in doctrine and government. The first board of Queen's had 37 members in addition to Governor Franklin and three other officials; 24 of the 37 were laymen—esquires, baronets, colonels—and 13 were ministers. This met the charter requirement that not more than one-third of the board might be clergymen. Geographically, the board was equally divided between New Jersey and New York, a fair reflection of the numbers and location of the Dutch settlements.

Each charter clearly states the purpose of the college: "the Education of Youth in the Learned Languages and in the Liberal Arts and Sciences." The phrasing is identical in both, except that the Queen's charter adds the words "and useful" after "Liberal." This additional adjective, though nobody thought of it at the time, proved broad enough a century later to justify the practical and vocational courses of instruction which came as a result of the Land Grant Act and marked the first steps in the process that was to make Rutgers the State University. The desirability of training ministers is also mentioned in the Queen's charter while that of the Princeton institution says not a word about this need. Both charters explicitly grant admission to all who qualify, regardless of their religious views or affiliations, and there is no denominational test for students or faculty. The Queen's charter did originally require that the president, who might or might not be a trustee, be a member of the Dutch Reformed Church, but this provision was allowed to lapse and was no longer in force when the last vestigial tie with the church was severed in 1909.

In view of the demonstrated religious zeal of the founders of both institutions, the liberal provisions and broadly tolerant tone of both charters might seem puzzling, were it not for two facts. In the first place, the Great Awakening which had precipitated the college movement was interdenominational and deprecated all sectarian narrowness. Furthermore it was not anti-intellectual, as revival movements often are, but was characterized by a very real concern for education. But there was still another reason for the inclusive and conciliatory language of the charters. Both groups of petitioners represented minorities, and it was by no means certain that the provincial authorities would grant their requests. The Presbyterians, especially, encountered opposition from Anglicans and Quakers, who largely constituted the ruling classes in colonial New Jersey. To placate this opposition and to gain status, they had to formulate their charter in the most liberal terms; as a matter of fact they based it upon the original Grant of Liberties of the Proprietors in 1665. Though this kind of opposition had subsided somewhat by the time the Queen's charter was being considered, it was still expedient to present the proposed college in the most favorable light. Language differences increased the difficulty here, for Dutch was still the principal medium of worship in the churches and, to a large extent, of communication in the home. This accounts for the otherwise unintelligible provision in the Queen's charter that the College must always maintain one professor "well versed in the English language." Probably no other state university has so firm a foundation for its English department.

The College of New Jersey had been functioning successfully for a quarter of a century and Queen's, with a more precarious hold on life, for less than a decade, when both had to face the shock of revolution and war. Neither could escape. Both Princeton and New Brunswick sat on the great highway between New York and Philadelphia, squarely in the path of the marching armies. From that morning in January, 1777, when Nassau Hall echoed to the thunder of the guns of the Battle of Princeton, to the day in late August, 1781, when General Washington, in a letter written at New Brunswick, directed Simeon DeWitt, chief geographer of the Army and a Queen's graduate, to survey the road to Yorktown, the two little Jersey college towns were rarely free from war's alarms.

Early in the quarrel with the mother country, the students, faculty, and administration of both institutions had taken the side of colonial rights and ultimately of Independence. Loyalists were few on either campus. At Nassau Hall, students whose parents had Tory leanings were ducked under the college pump and otherwise molested. If such behavior seems odd, inasmuch as the propertied classes, who could afford to send their sons to college, were usually conservative and on the side of the established order, it must be remembered that the supporters of both Queen's and Nassau Hall were non-English minorities with no built-in loyalty to the British Crown. Well-to-do Anglicans and Quakers with Loyalist leanings had little interest in either institution, having schools of their own in New York and Philadelphia. This is not to imply that the Scotch and the Dutch carried New Jersey for Independence. The Dutch element, apart from its college, was divided on the issue, while the Scottish Presbyterians were influenced by many transplanted New Englanders in their midst who favored separation. Yet the stand of the two colleges was unmistakable.

From the beginning, New Brunswick was a center of revolutionary activity. The first extra-legal Provincial Assembly met there to condemn the coercive acts of Parliament and elect members to the Continental Congress. Queen's College shared the sentiments of this assembly. Jacob Hardenbergh, at the time Chairman of the Board of Trustees, came out openly for Independence and was a member of the later convention which framed the first State constitution. *Persona non grata* to the British, he lived a life of harassment throughout the war, and his church at Raritan was burned by Simcoe's raiders. During the winter of 1779 Washington had his Headquarters next door to Hardenbergh's parsonage and the two men became friends. At the end of his stay the Commander-in-Chief addressed a deeply appreciative letter to the domine and the elders and deacons of his church. Frederick Frelinghuysen, who was the sole tutor

—that means the entire faculty—of the College at the opening of the war, promptly enlisted on the side of Independence. He fought in most of the campaigns in New Jersey and rose to the rank of major-general. In later years a United States senator and a life-long trustee of Queen's, Frelinghuysen had imbibed revolutionary sentiments in his undergraduate days at Princeton where he had learned patriotism as well as Greek and where he chose as the theme of his commencement oration, "The Utility of American Manufactures."

The role of Princeton in the Revolution is part of the Nation's history. Every school child knows of Washington's signal victory there, a week after his equally brilliant exploit at Trenton, and of the effect of this double blow in reviving the morale of the patriot army and saving what had almost become a lost cause. In the course of the battle, American artillery bombarded Nassau Hall, where some of Cornwallis' troops had taken refuge, and one shot tore through the portrait of George II, from whom the original College charter had emanated. But the triumphant climax for the College came at the end of the war, when the Continental Congress fled from Philadelphia to Princeton to escape some mutinous troops and continued its sessions there. For a few weeks the little town was the Capital of the United States. It was in Nassau Hall that General Washington was received by the Congress and congratulated upon the successful completion of the fight for independence. Commencement that year, 1783, saw Washington in the audience, along with the French Minister, seven signers of the Declaration of Independence, eleven future signers of the Constitution, and many members of Congress.

No account of Princeton in the Revolution would be complete without mention of one of the College's great presidents, John Witherspoon, whose term of office covered the entire revolutionary period, from 1768 to 1794. A Scottish theologian and a scholar of international renown, Witherspoon was persuaded to come to

America and throw in his lot with the little college in the new world. Here, besides serving as a unifying influence in the factional disputes of the Church, he became almost immediately a leader in the movement for colonial rights. A stimulating teacher, Witherspoon introduced contemporary topics into his lectures on moral philosophy, a flexible subject that lent itself to such treatment, and encouraged his students to discuss the burning issues of the day in the light of contemporary theories of the rights of man. As might be expected, these "progressive" ideas of the President met with considerable disapproval among conservatives in the colony. One such critic, who attended the commencement of 1772, thought it highly improper for the graduating class to express what seemed to him daring opinions on questions relating to the British Constitution, for "it leads them to speak of what they know not." * It was probably not the first and certainly not the last time that anxious conservatives have expressed alarm over manifestations of radicalism on American campuses.

Carrying these views beyond the campus into the community, Witherspoon became a leader in the movement for Independence, a member of the Continental Congress and a signer of the Declaration of Independence, and one of the most honored citizens of New Jersey. His growing prominence in State and National affairs, together with his role of peacemaker between the evangelical and conservative wings of the Presbyterian Church, gave his college a national reputation. Wherever the Scotch-Irish settled—from New York to Georgia and from the seaboard to the Ohio—the College of New Jersey was well and favorably known. Not only the Scotch-Irish, but prominent families of other national and denominational origins sent their sons to Nassau Hall. The roster of students in Witherspoon's day included Lees, Livingstons, Madisons, Morrisses, Randolphs,

* Thomas J. Wertenbaker, *Princeton 1746-1896* (Princeton, 1946), 100.

and Van Rensselaers. Among those who sat at Witherspoon's feet were a future president of the United States, a vice-president, ten Cabinet officers, 21 United States senators, 39 members of the House of Representatives, three Supreme Court justices, and twelve governors.

The war was not all glory. It brought hardships and losses to both colleges. The records for those years, though damaged and incomplete, depict a hazardous, fly-by-night existence. When Cornwallis' troops approached in the autumn of 1776, classes were disrupted and the students dispersed, both in New Brunswick and Princeton. A school of sorts, known as the Queen's Grammar School, was maintained throughout the war years in Raritan, where a couple of tutors taught elementary branches and apparently a few college classes as well. A commencement was held in New Brunswick in 1778, and by 1782 Queen's College was again carrying on after a fashion in its old building, which was much the worse for neglect and war damage. Meanwhile, precious funds had melted away in the wartime inflation, and the College was left with "a naked charter and little else." * Scarcely thirty students all told are known to have been enrolled in all those years.

In a like manner, the students of Nassau Hall, dispersed by the British, reassembled now and then in small groups through the ensuing years. Some lodged in town, others risked the unheated rooms of the dilapidated College building. In the president's house a professor and a tutor conducted classes in a desultory fashion, and President Witherspoon himself, when home from sessions of the Congress, gave an occasional lecture. Nassau Hall was occupied first by the British, then by the Continentals; they were equally destructive. Horses were stabled in the basement, windows were broken, woodwork was ripped up, plaster cracked and crumbled. Late in the war Witherspoon secured a Congressional appropriation of almost twenty thousands dollars for repairs,

* William H. S. Demarest, *A History of Rutgers College 1766-1924* (New Brunswick, 1924), 141.

but before these could be completed, the value of the funds had shrunk to five cents on the dollar. Still, the College resumed activities in the half-wrecked, scarcely habitable building, and by the end of the fighting in 1782 was again enrolling 40 students.

Sustained by the same kind of sacrifice and devotion that marked their beginnings, the two New Jersey colleges somehow carried on and survived the Revolutionary War.

II

THE STRUGGLE FOR SURVIVAL

EMERGING FROM THE War of Independence poor in purse and low in morale, the two New Jersey colleges gradually regained momentum as they moved into the nineteenth century. It was not all smooth sailing. On the National scene they now found themselves in competition not only with their pre-Revolutionary neighbors but with many new institutions. The first half of the nineteenth century saw the erection of hundreds of colleges and schools that aspired to become colleges. They were founded by the missionary zeal of churches or the local patriotism of growing towns, often with the same naive confidence and lack of sound financial support as western townsites and wildcat banks. American higher education was competitive like American economic life and, in the absence of any central control or planning, almost anarchic.

Under such conditions, progress and expansion were by no means assured, even for pre-Revolutionary establishments like Nassau Hall and Queen's. On the contrary, both had repeated sinking spells and protracted low periods. This was particularly true of Queen's, which almost went under on two different occasions, suspending classes from 1795 to 1807, and again from 1817 to 1825. Just before the first lapse a serious attempt was made to unite the two schools. A joint committee selected from the two boards of trustees proposed a merger in which Queen's was to become the sole preparatory school, while all the college work was to be offered at Princeton. None but inhabitants of New Jersey were to be eligible for membership in the governing body of the united institution. The Princeton authorities, though favorably inclined, postponed action, and before they could reconvene the trustees of Queen's rejected the proposal by a vote of eight to seven. Had one of those votes gone the other way, the history of higher education in New Jersey might have taken a different turn.

Soon after this abortive attempt at union—in 1795, when the graduating class numbered two—Queen's suspended its college work and only the Grammar School continued to function. The latter, a well-managed preparatory school, gained a reputation beyond the borders of the State and drew students from as far away as Tennessee. It also tried to keep alive a partial freshman and sophomore college program. In 1807 the full college was revived, owing largely to the efforts of one of the trustees, Judge Andrew Kirkpatrick, Chief Justice of New Jersey. It was at this time that the first academic building, Old Queen's, was erected. This was a long step forward, for it gave the college a home and ended its peripatetic period of shuffling from one private house to another. On land acquired for a campus in the north end of New Brunswick, the building was begun in 1809 and occupied, though still unfinished, in 1811. It was designed by John McComb, architect of New York's City Hall. Like Nassau Hall fifty years earlier, Old Queen's was stripped of the decorative features in the original design; though this was done for reasons of economy, it probably resulted in a more attractive building. The final cost was thirty thousand dollars.

In 1817 funds gave out again, and for the second time college activities came to an end, the hiatus lasting eight years this time. In 1825, the proceeds of a lottery together with a gift of five thousand dollars from Colonel Henry Rutgers, a prominent citizen of

New York City, put the college back on its feet, and it has continued in operation without further interruption from that day to this. In recognition of the colonel's gift and perhaps in lively anticipation of more, the trustees changed the name, in 1825, from Queen's to Rutgers College.

The plight of the College of New Jersey at Princeton was never as serious as that of Queen's, but it too suffered repeated setbacks. Recovering after the Revolution with 40 undergraduates, where pre-war enrollments had run as high as a hundred-twenty, it soon equaled and then surpassed the earlier figure. For a variety of reasons there followed decades of violent fluctuation both in size and income. The post-war generation of students was less tractable—less hopefully pious, in the language of their elders—than their predecessors. The young men had caught the spirit of the new Republic: triumphant, bumptious, and given to bluster and self-aggrandizement; faculty and administration too often failed to understand the change or to deal wisely with the new breed of student. To compound the difficulties, there were disagreements among Presbyterian leaders about the purpose of higher education, and the conservative element was gaining control. Because of these constricted viewpoints Nassau Hall was losing its national character, at least for the time being, and shrinking into a provincial mold. Southern students especially were beginning to by-pass Princeton and go on to New Haven. Later, after abolitionism spread in New England, Princeton was to recover its hegemony. In 1830, Yale had 56 students from below the Mason-Dixon line, Princeton 22; but ten years later Yale had only 40, representing about ten percent of its total student body, while Princeton had 94, about forty percent of the total. *

In the face of all these difficulties, student enrollment, which had approached two hundred in 1806, dropped to 71 in 1827. The income from all sources in that

* These figures were taken from the *American Almanac and Repository of Useful Knowledge* for the years 1830 and 1860.

NASSAU HALL IN 1837

Nassau Hall, as it appeared from 1804 to 1855. After the fire of 1802, the famous building was restored by Benjamin H. Latrobe, considered by many the "greatest architect of his generation in America."

year was $6,147; expenditures were $6,900. To meet the financial crisis and to recover their shrinking share of the academic market, the trustees reduced the tuition fee to twenty dollars a year and board to two dollars a week. They also reduced faculty salaries. From the low point of 1827 the fortunes of the college slowly improved; enrollments increased again, and by 1860 the student body numbered three hundred. Even in these undistinguished decades, generally considered its most mediocre period, Nassau Hall managed to turn out a respectable number of future congressmen, state governors, and college presidents.

A quantitative comparison of the two New Jersey institutions with other American colleges in the first half of the nineteenth century shows neither of them among the leaders, though Princeton had begun to make its way toward the top by 1860. The table on page 22 is based on compilations made in the *American Almanac and Repository of Useful Knowledge,* for 1830 and 1860 respectively; these in turn rest upon statistical information furnished for the preceding year by the colleges listed.

Prominent among the factors that hampered the growth of the two New Jersey colleges was their equivocal relationship to the church. Until this was resolved, neither could move forward with confidence and singleness of purpose. Legally, by the provisions of their charters, both were entirely free of denominational control, being governed by independent, self-perpetuating boards of trustees. Actually, both had been called into existence by Christian leaders, most of them clergymen, who thought of them primarily as training schools for future ministers of the Gospel, in the Presbyterian or the Reformed Church. Clergymen, though not in the majority, dominated both boards of trustees. In the first third of the nineteenth century, church control of both institutions was, if anything, intensified; the next thirty years saw a gradual relaxation of these controls until, by about 1870, they had been largely eliminated, and

STUDENT ENROLLMENT IN AMERICAN COLLEGES

1830

Name	*Rank*	*Faculty*	*Students*	*Library Volumes*
Yale	1	16	324	8,500
Harvard	2	15	254	30,000
Union	3	9	223	5,000
Amherst	4	9	211	2,300
Virginia	5	8	131	8,000
Dartmouth	6	8	128	3,500
Columbia (1831)	7	6	124	
Princeton	16	6	71	8,000
Rutgers	17	6	63	
Pennsylvania	24	5	50	

1860

Name	*Rank*	*Faculty*	*Students*	*Library Volumes*
Yale	1	21	502	67,000
North Carolina	2	15	450	21,000
Virginia	3	14	417	30,000
Harvard	4	24	409	123,400
Union	5	15	326	15,500
Dartmouth	6	16	304	33,699
Princeton	7	17	300	21,400
Columbia	14	12	173	14,000
Pennsylvania	15	12	129	5,100
Rutgers	16	8	116	12,000

both Princeton and Rutgers emerged as independent secular colleges.

To label this development as merely another chapter in the long struggle between theology and science would be a distortion, yet there was that element—not that the preachers were opposed to the secular branches as such or were setting up a polarity between piety and intellect. On the contrary, most of the Presbyterian and Reformed church leaders, educated men themselves, were hospitable to literature and science. Their science, however, had no autonomous existence but was justified only as a handmaiden to religion, illustrating the ways of God with men; and they wished to see it practiced within the bounds of Calvinistic orthodoxy. They were doomed to disappointment. The free human spirit has always tended, with incorrigible persistence, to break out of the confining orthodoxies of the time and to chart new courses in the endless search for truth. And so college professors and presidents, while faithful to the Church in their fashion, were perennially finding themselves in the bad graces of the church's conservative clerical leadership. It was not easy to keep classroom activities in constant alignment with the eternal verities of Calvin and Knox.

Concern for the faith, coupled with chronic suspicion of what the professors of arts and sciences were up to, expressed itself in various ways on both campuses. When the Reverend John H. Livingston, biblical scholar, professor of divinity, and outstanding leader in the Reformed church, became the president of Queen's College, in 1810, he found a lively interest in science, particularly chemistry, in both College and town. Annoyed at this overemphasis on the secular, he exclaimed: "The chemists talk of their oxygen, hydrogen, and nitrogen. Fools! Fools! What do they know about it? After all it is nothing but matter." * Again, the zeal for orthodoxy might take other forms. When an architect at Princeton in 1847 submitted a cruciform design for a campus chapel, conservative trustees protested at this subtle invasion of the minds of the young with most un-Presbyterian notions of ritual and liturgy.

Throughout the protracted struggle between ecclesiastics and academicians there were able and honorable men on both sides, but the Church wielded the bigger club: it was the principal source of income. Without regular collections and drives for funds among the church membership, neither college could have survived. Such drives, to be successful, had to be sanctioned by the church authorities, and they were not slow in demanding concessions and guarantees in return. In 1808, the Presbyterian General Assembly, saddened at the increasing worldliness of the College of New Jersey and the

* William H. S. Demarest, *A History of Rutgers College 1766-1924* (New Brunswick, 1924), 227.

decreasing number of its graduates who entered the ministry, resolved to establish a theological seminary and to transfer the support to the Church to the new institution. The seminary was to be allowed to house and feed its students in Nassau Hall, to use the library there, and to erect such buildings as it chose on the college campus. It chose, eventually, to establish its own campus some distance away—perhaps to escape worldly contamination. Trustees of the College were also, in considerable numbers, members of the board of trustees or of the faculty of the Seminary. Thirty-six men, between 1812 and 1868, served in such dual roles. While there were always prominent members of other denominations among Princeton's leaders, and while no formal religious test was ever imposed on either faculty or students, prospective candidates for professorships or for vacancies on the board of trustees usually found it advantageous, whatever their other qualifications, to be known as staunch Presbyterians.

At Rutgers, the Synod of the Reformed Church agreed to pay the salary of its president, who was also to be professor of divinity, in return for a controlling voice in the selection of faculty and trustees. The first president to operate under this arrangement was Dr. Livingston, who took office in 1810. Leaving a flourishing congregation in New York City and a salary of two thousand and five hundred dollars, Livingston was promised one thousand and four hundred dollars per annum and the rent of a house in New Brunswick. He actually received $771.86 in two years. In 1825 the college, now Rutgers, actually deeded its main building, Old Queen's, to the Reformed Church which thereupon paid off a college debt of four thousand dollars and collected an additional four thousand and eight hundred dollars for current expenses. At this time, in the words of one New Jersey historian, Rutgers "was practically a theological seminary with a literary course." * In fact,

* Nelson R. Burr, *Education in New Jersey, 1630-1871* (Princeton, 1942), 27.

both Rutgers and Princeton were virtually mortgaged to their theological schools.

Then the tide turned. Beginning in 1839, the president of Rutgers was no longer required to be professor of theology. In the following year, the first layman, the Hon. A. Bruyn Hasbrouck, former member of Congress, was elected president. In 1856, the seminary evacuated the college campus altogether and moved its own quarters, where it flourishes today; soon after, the college bought its building back. At about this time too, following some unfortunate misunderstandings and much recrimination, "the title, Rutgers College, disappeared from the order of business in the minutes of the General Synod." * And so, its indenture to the Church at an end, Rutgers emerged as an independent college. Princeton's emancipation from church control was not completed until the last decade of the nineteenth century, in the administration of President Patton.

The circumstance that contributed more than any other to this emancipation was the gradual achievement of financial stability. It was a slow and painful process in which virtually everyone connected with the institution was involved—trustees, faculty, even students. But the main burden fell upon the president. This was true of American colleges generally. Collecting funds was not a duty prescribed in the charter, but it was inescapable. The president might be a reputable scholar and an excellent teacher, and was indeed expected to carry his share of the teaching load, but the pleasant groves of academe were not for him. Sooner or later, he had to leave his books and lectures and take to the road to "sell" the college. He still does.

John Witherspoon was hardly settled in Princeton when he had to start out on his travels. Using summer vacations, he criss-crossed the Colonies from Boston to Williamsburg promoting the new college and soliciting funds, while other agents tapped the Presbyterian com-

* William H. S. Demarest, *A History of Rutgers College 1766-1924* (New Brunswick, 1924), 359.

munities in the deep South. In similar fashion, representatives of Nassau Hall and of Queen's sailed to England, Scotland, and the Netherlands, to plead their cause. But when Witherspoon tried Europe at the close of the War for Independence, he failed to collect anything in England, for understandable reasons, and was warned by Benjamin Franklin not to come to France at all. Jacob R. Hardenbergh, first president of Queen's, worked equally hard, but with far less success, to keep his college solvent. Financial worries broke him down and he died in 1790 with his salary £330 in arrears. As his part in a fund-raising campaign among the Reformed churches, Ira Condict, Hardenbergh's successor, walked from house to house in New Brunswick for contributions which ranged from a shilling to a dollar. Thus the presidents of both schools set a pattern from which few of their successors could entirely escape. Discouraging, too, was the fact that returns often lagged far behind the goals set. At Princeton in the 1830's an ambitious program was launched to raised a fund of one hundred thousand dollars, toward which even faculty members pledged as much as one thousand dollars. But the Panic of 1837 played hob with the subscriptions and the actual sum collected melted down to less than nine thousand dollars, of which four thousand dollars went as commission to the agent who had managed the campaign.

Funds thus laboriously collected were subject to many stresses and strains. Both colleges lost most of their accumulated funds in the currency inflation of the Revolution and the period of Confederation; like merchants, farmers, and laborers, they were affected by every turn of the business cycle. Unforeseen calamities—acts of God—could wreck the best financial program and play havoc with the thriftiest academic housekeeping. Nassau Hall was gutted by fire on two occasions, in 1802 and 1855. The trustees did not think the first an act of God, but suspended five students as suspected incendiaries. Whether guilty or not, the five were also charged with vice and irreligion, and the College was considered well rid of them. In the second restoration the building was made fireproof as far as possible. Rutgers was spared such disastrous fires. With the exception of New Jersey Hall, which caught fire once but unfortunately resisted destruction, and the old Ballantine Gymnasium, it lost no major building.

Public support through taxes for private church-related institutions was not part of New Jersey's practice, though it happened sporadically in other states. There was one exception. The College of New Jersey asked for public funds to repair the damage to Nassau Hall in the Battle of Princeton, and the Continental Congress made partial amends, unfortunately in inflated currency. After considerable delay, the State Legislature voted forty-eight hundred dollars for partial reimbursement in 1795. But when most of the members who had voted for the appropriation were defeated for re-election, no further grants were made. In public addresses in the 1830's alumni asked for legislative aid to enlarge the faculty and permit expansion into a university; and a speaker at a meeting of the New Jersey Historical Society in 1846 came out strongly for financial support by the State to both Princeton and Rutgers. But nothing came of any of this. Princeton received no further support from the Legislature, and the first direct appropriation to Rutgers was not made until 1890, when that college had already entered upon the course that was eventually to make it the State University.

A form of money-raising that required the sanction of the state was the lottery, a device widely used, as bingo is today, to aid education and religion in the eighteenth century. Very early in its history, the College of New Jersey launched a lottery for which Benjamin Franklin printed eight thousand tickets to be sold in New York, Philadelphia, and Boston. New Jersey law forbade their sale. Though it met with some disapproval in church circles, this lottery yielded a profit which gave President Burr "such pleasure that his spirits were quite revived."* Queen's tried a lottery on several occasions, the first in 1812 as part of a campaign to pay for the new building. For this one, fifteen thousand tickets were offered at seven dollars each. There were over five thousand prizes, the largest of twenty-five hundred dollars, most of them ten dollars. The fragmentary records and the amateur bookkeeping of that day make it difficult to determine how much the college actually profited from the venture. Estimates range from nothing to eleven thousand dollars of the twenty thousand expected. Ten years later, the Legislature grudgingly consented to another try. This time a professional firm took over the promotion and Rutgers' final share was not quite twenty-five thousand dollars out of a total of three hundred thirty-seven thousand dollars which the public subscribed. Amid charges of abuse and legislative recriminations, lotteries gradually fell into disfavor. They were unprofitable for the college and increasingly considered unethical.**

The greatest contribution to ultimate financial stability came in the form of gifts from former students. In 1826, Princeton graduates formed an alumni association, and Rutgers graduates organized similarly in 1832. They were not unique; college alumni associations came to be a favorite American device for supporting higher education by combining individual independence with voluntary association for the common good. European universities had nothing like it. The announced purpose of the founders at Princeton was "to promote the interests of the college and the friendly intercourse of its graduates." James Madison was elected president. The Rutgers alumni began by agitating for the needs of education in New Jersey and by suggesting, among other things, a nation-wide association of college graduates. Their first tangible contribution was a gift of two thousand dollars

* Thomas J. Wertenbaker, *Princeton 1746-1896* (Princeton, 1946), 32.

** Philip G. Nordell, "The Rutgers Lotteries," *Journal of the Rutgers University Library*, XVI, No. 1 (1952).

A PRINT OF THE RUTGERS CAMPUS ABOUT 1844

Old Queen's, built in 1809, and Van Nest Hall proudly carry on; but the old President's House, on the right, has been recently torn down.

toward the erection of Van Nest Hall, the second college building, in 1846.

At Princeton, finances improved from the time the organized alumni took a hand. Projected amounts grew larger and larger, and though the campaign results still fell short of the goals, the habit of giving was established. The price exacted in return was increased participation of the alumni in the affairs of Alma Mater, which in turn meant alumni advisory councils and eventually alumni membership on the board of trustees. It was a generous participation on the whole, though it could be critical too. From this time on, the presidents of Princeton and Rutgers, as of American colleges and universities in general, have had an organized alumni looking over their shoulders and displaying a concern that can be embarrassing but is also, especially in times of crisis, a tower of strength.

III

GLIMPSES OF TWO CLASSICAL COLLEGES

WHAT WENT ON in the classrooms of the college in Princeton and the college in New Brunswick in those early years? We know a good deal about the curricula of American colleges in general. They all—with occasional exceptions—taught the same things in the same way. Their course of study, brought over from Europe, was known as the liberal arts and sciences; historically, it is often referred to as "the classical tradition." As old as Western civilization itself, the arts and sciences have undergone many changes in content and form, yet underneath all change a persistent idea has remained intact. In all ages the pursuit of the liberal arts has meant the attempt of men to discover, by the free use of their faculties, something of the nature and meaning of the universe, man's place in it, and the highest values to which human life can attain. Put in another way, the arts and sciences were those subjects of general interest and importance that were held to be the indispensable intellectual equipment of an educated person. In form and content they go back to Aristotle, that intellectual giant of the ancient world to whom we owe both substance and method of our thought to such a degree that even the categories under which we organize our knowledge, the "ologies" of our college catalogues, are largely his formulation.

This classical course of study came to Harvard and

William and Mary, and through them to all American colleges, from the European universities of the Middle Ages via Cambridge and Oxford. Its chief ingredients when it reached the new world were three: the Aristotelian philosophy rendered palatable for Christian consumption by the Medieval Schoolmen; polite letters, both Latin and Greek, the contribution of the Italian Renaissance; and mathematics, a reflection of the seventeenth century's increasing preoccupation with science. Its purpose, in the language of the Harvard Charter of 1650, was "the advancement of all good literature, artes and Sciences" in the framework of eternity: "The maine end of [the student's] life and studies is, to know God and Jesus Christ which is eternall life." In proclaiming these goals the Charter spoke not only for Harvard but, as it turned out, for the oldtime American college in general. A president of Columbia, a contemporary of Princeton's Maclean and Rutgers' Frelinghuysen, was to rephrase them over two hundred years later: "Here in college is to be fashioned, in the highest attainable perfection, the scholar, the citizen, the good man, the Christian gentleman."*

Princeton and Rutgers were trying to do precisely that. The actual course of study which they, like other American colleges, constructed out of these inherited cultural materials, took shape as follows. Freshmen and sophomores spent most of their classroom time translating Latin and Greek classics and acquiring, it was hoped, a disciplined mind and a free spirit in the process. The remainder of the first two years was given to rhetoric, mathematics, and "natural philosophy"—which was lectures, sometimes accompanied by simple experimental demonstrations, in the rudiments of physics and chemistry. When such an embryonic science course, usually considered one of the frills, was assigned to a clergyman-professor who knew little about it, heroic measures were

* The Harvard Charter is cited in Samuel E. Morison, *The Founding of Harvard College* (Cambridge, 1935), 160. The president of Columbia was Charles King, and the words are from his Inaugural Address in 1849.

called for. There is a story of one such pedagogue—not at Rutgers or Princeton—who rose to the emergency, when his little chemical experiments misfired, by reassuring the class through the ensuing havoc: "Nevertheless, young gentlemen, the principle remains firm as the everlasting hills."

In the program of the junior and senior years, the study of classical languages tapered off to make way for logic, metaphysics, ethics, and polemical lectures on the evidences of Christianity, the last usually taught by the president. Smatterings of modern languages, history, political economy, botany, and geology rounded out the program. This was the nineteenth-century version of a liberal education. Inflexible and irreducible, it was required of all candidates for the degree. There was no such thing as shifting to a curriculum in business administration or physical education if the triple demands of language, mathematics, and philosophy proved too formidable. The student took the whole program, neat, or he did not graduate.

In fact, he could not get into college without considerable grounding in the classics, and admissions practices were designed to make sure that he had it. Here again, Princeton and Rutgers were no exception; their statutes and catalogues make this perfectly clear. Candidates for admission were examined, orally as a rule, for their ability to translate Caesar, Cicero, and Virgil into English, and then, in reverse, to translate any English passage selected by the professor into grammatical Latin. They had to translate passages from the four Gospels from the Greek and to do arithmetic problems including the rule of proportion and vulgar and decimal fractions. Later in the century, elementary algebra was added to the admission requirements. "Reading English with propriety," the Princeton regulation went on to explain, "spelling the English language and writing it without grammatical errors" were taken for granted. This held for Rutgers too, even though the constituency of that college had originally spoken Dutch.

Thorough enough as far as they went, these entrance examinations seem to have been administered in a casual manner. There was no bookkeeping involving high school credits, there were no aptitude tests or College Entrance Boards. It was fairly common for applicants at Princeton to skip the freshman year and be admitted to the sophomore class. But there is no evidence that either New Jersey college followed the practice of an early president of Yale who inquired into the financial status of the applicant. If well-heeled, the student was registered as a freshman, but if there was financial stringency he might, if otherwise acceptable, be admitted to the sophomore class. Sloppy and inefficient, is our verdict on such admission practices today. Yet in the early nineteenth century such flexible casualness was not entirely without reason and benefit. There were no standard secondary schools insuring equal training, and applicants came unevenly prepared. In such a situation an understanding professor could deal wisely with each prospective student according to his individual needs and capacities.

If there was any deviation from the norm in the curricula of the two New Jersey colleges it was in the direction of a stronger emphasis on mathematics and science. In the case of Princeton, this emphasis grew out of its early association with the higher schools maintained by Dissenters in Britain. The liveliest centers of education in eighteenth-century England, these dissenting academies kept in much closer touch with current scientific developments than did the complacent and stagnating universities at Oxford and Cambridge. It is not surprising, therefore, to find a professor of chemistry on the faculty at Princeton as early as 1795, or to read of Joseph Henry's exciting course in physics there three decades later. Long before John Dewey, Henry "motivated" his students by demonstrating the "life-adjustment" value of his subject. His demonstrations included, among other things, a wire strung from his classroom to his home, over which he telegraphed his wife when he was ready to come home for lunch. Rutgers was favorably known for its work in mathematics, especially when Robert Adrain, an outstanding teacher and a productive scholar, conducted that department. Chemistry appeared by name in the Rutgers catalogue in 1833, geology in 1841. Geological Hall, with its valuable collection of fossils and specimens, was erected in 1872. Van Nest Hall, the second building built on the campus, contained a laboratory, unusual for a college in 1847. It was Van Nest, too, that later housed the Agricultural Experiment Station, which was to have such a far-reaching influence on the destiny of the future State University.

In the main, however, and in spite of these minor variations, Princeton and Rutgers hewed to the line of the classical tradition and opposed all radical proposals for broadening or diversifying the course of study. The presidents of both lined up squarely with the Yale faculty when the latter issued its famous Report of 1829, which uncompromisingly restated the faith of the conservatives in the disciplinary values of the inherited curriculum as good for all time. A quarter-century later, John Maclean summed up the accepted view on his accession to the Princeton presidency: "We shall not aim at innovations. . . . No chimerical experiments in education have ever had the least countenance here." * While fringe subjects would be given the attention they deserved, the core curriculum would continue to be religion, philosophy, Greek, Latin, and mathematics, and the ultimate objective would remain mental discipline.

Not very exciting intellectual fare, it would seem in retrospect. Nor was there much enrichment in the college libraries. Here too, classical titles predominated, along with theological treatises, and what was even more discouraging, the books were almost inaccessible. The Rutgers Library was open from eight-thirty to nine on Saturday mornings, when a student supervised the drawing of books. This practice was begun in 1825. At Prince-

* John Maclean, *History of the College of New Jersey* (Philadelphia, 1877), II, 421, 427.

A CHEMISTRY CLASS AT RUTGERS, ABOUT 1885

Professor Peter T. Austen is seated at the right, Professor F. A. Wilber at the left.

ton, as late as 1868, the Library was open one hour a week for the same purpose. Students were not encouraged to read or browse there, for this might distract them from their studies.

At its best, the American classical college did give the serious student the habit of critical thinking in a limited field, and a fair grounding in ancient languages and in philosophy. Among the subjects most likely to strike fire was the senior course in mental and moral philosophy, usually given by the president. In this last confrontation before turning his students loose in the world, the president had the chance to tie the four years together and provide them with some kind of a binding philosophy. "To unite together piety and literature" was Witherspoon's way of putting it. Flexible in form and content, this course could, in the hands of a scholar of breadth and understanding, become the culminating experience of college years. Such a man was Samuel Stanhope Smith, son-in-law of and successor to Witherspoon. Smith's lectures to the senior class, which were later published, included not only formal metaphysics and ethics, but discussions of current economic and political issues, social and psychological problems, in short the rudiments of what has since become the broad field of the social sciences. Among the many topics touched on in his lectures are the relative influence of heredity and environment on human evolution (he does not use that word); democracy and aristocracy (in which he takes issue with Aristotle); free trade, and freedom of religion. It must have been an exciting course and still makes good reading today.* It was too exciting for the clerical governors of Nassau Hall, who scented heresy in the president's free-wheeling discussions of dangerous topics; so they curbed his authority and maneuvered him into resigning his office. His successor redirected the course into narrower and safer channels. A similar fate befell

* Samuel Stanhope Smith, *The Lectures Delivered . . . in the College of New Jersey on . . . Moral and Political Philosophy* (2 vols.; Trenton, 1812).

THE PRINCETON FACULTY IN 1867

President John Maclean and his entire Princeton faculty, 1867-1868. They stand before the house of Professor Arnold H. Guyot on Nassau Street.

a professor of Greek who had penetrated beyond grammar and syntax into the ideas of the classical writers, to the amazement and delight of his students. Sternly admonished by the president to return to his aorists and participles, he stood his ground, tried to justify his more enlightened practice, and was asked to resign. The atmosphere at Rutgers was no different. When for example George William Hill, distinguished mathematician and astronomer, was an undergraduate there, he tried to push his studies beyond the bounds of the prescribed curriculum, but the faculty with one exception firmly discouraged such a breach of decorum. This was typical.

Caught in this theological and intellectual strait-jacket, the average professor, overloaded as he was with teaching hours and disciplinary chores, tended to limit himself to mechanics and routine, no matter how dull and how exasperating to his students. Yet each faculty continued to produce stimulating teachers along with the martinets and literalists who made up the majority. Such rare individuals, those who combined genuine scholarship with a gift of expression and human sympathy, could make the dullest subject come to life, thereby transforming the drab classroom into a dwelling-place of light and achieving that most exhilarating of experiences: an honest meeting of minds. Fortunate the students who encountered at least one such teacher and course, for they remembered it the rest of their lives as the thing that had made college worth while.

The actual quality of the educational experience at Princeton and Rutgers when compared to that at rival institutions is difficult to determine, for there were no nationally fixed standards. Fragmentary evidence indicates that students moved freely from one college to another, and this is not surprising since the course of study was everywhere the same and the faculty members had had the same classical-theological training. On one occasion twelve students who had withdrawn from Yale, "encouraged by the authorities," came to Rutgers. According to one of the twelve, the transferees found their new Alma Mater very pleasant, for it had competent instructors who treated the students with kindness and respect. One would like to hear the Yale version of this exodus. A Rutgers graduate of 1847 who went to Harvard for an extra year of study reported that he could hold his own with the Harvard students in everything but the writing of themes.*

Another way to assess the range and quality of the old classical education is to look at the course examinations. Some of these have survived. For a number of years the annual Princeton catalogue reprinted the final-examination questions given to the senior class of the previous year. Questions such as these might have been asked at Rutgers, or Yale, or any one of a score of colleges. Here are some examples from the *Calendar of the College of New Jersey, 1870-1871,* a year when the classical college was at the height of its powers. In that year all seniors at Princeton were examined in Latin, Greek, chemistry, political economy, religion and science (i.e. the reconciliation of the two). Mathematics had apparently been disposed of at the end of the junior year; an examination in English literature from Chaucer to Tennyson was added in 1871. In Latin, the *pièce de résistance* was a passage from Quintilian which had to be translated into idiomatic English, then analyzed for syntax, derivations, subjunctives, and kinds of clauses. Questions on Quintilian's life, and an essay on the history of the Greek and Latin verb, with derivations from the Sanskrit, completed the examination in the ancient languages. Some of the questions in the other fields were as follows:

In chemistry: A pound of marble contains how much oxygen? Explain the preparation and uses of H_2S. If ten grams of iron rust, it is then what and how much? *In ethics:* Define conscience, how far it is cognitive

* William H. S. Demarest, *A History of Rutgers College 1766-1924* (New Brunswick, 1924), 315, 341.

and emotional. . . . Define truth. . . . Explain professional ethics, especially as related to the various obligations of lawyers.

In political economy: Explain value, utility, price, wealth, the rise and fall of prices in relation to supply and demand. State the various modes of restricting the freedom of labor, and explain the effects of bounties, special taxes, trade unions, and other forms of such restriction.

In history: Define civilization. . . . What were the causes of the fall of the Roman Empire? What was the effect of the Treaty of Westphalia on the international system of Europe? How did American civilization differ in its origin from European?

In religion and science: How does physical science show that there is an intelligent Author of Nature? How does physiology and psychology show the probability of a future life?

Any judgment of the quality of this examination as compared to present-day requirements would be difficult and also unfair, for other presuppositions prevail today. The chemistry questions seem rather elementary. Political economy was straight Manchester theory with a (possibly) unconscious anti-labor bias. History was not mere chronology but dealt with causes and results; the questions include some old chestnuts that are still in circulation. Ethics and metaphysics were quite theoretical except for that reference to lawyers. The subject of religion and science, with its loaded questions, was based on President McCosh's lectures on the evidences of Christianity. Latin and Greek are harder to compare because no comparison is possible with what no longer exists. While there are still competent departments of the classical languages both at Princeton and Rutgers, not a college senior in a thousand could tackle those questions today, for in most American colleges the subject is moribund.

To appreciate the impact of this course of study on the mind of the student we must know something of college life in general and the daily round of campus activities. It must be remembered that college students were several years younger than they are today. The average age of entering students was fourteen to fifteen years, instead of seventeen to eighteen. This made them no older than high school sophomores of today, and accounts in part for the paternal regime in force in nearly all American colleges of that day. The regime was more complete at Princeton where all students lived on campus in Nassau Hall and, as numbers grew, in East and West College. Rutgers students lived with families in New Brunswick and later in the century in fraternity houses, for Old Queen's was a classroom building and had living quarters only for faculty members. The first dormitory on the Rutgers campus was Winants Hall, built in 1890 to accommodate 85 students.

At Nassau Hall the day began at five in the morning, six in winter, when the students were roused by trumpets blown in the corridors. The college bell had proved ineffectual. Immediately upon rising they filed into the unheated prayer hall for morning devotions. These could become an ordeal, "the mornings being very cold and the tutors praying very long."* A study hour followed, lasting until breakfast at half-past seven. This consisted of bread and butter with milk or cider. Dinner, at noon, was a more substantial hot meal, supper was like breakfast. Students protested, of course, and occasionally rebelled against the meager and unpalatable fare; complaining about food has been the prerogative of students ever since the Middle Ages. The rare youth who admitted that he liked the meals was not popular with his

* Thomas J. Wertenbaker, *Princeton 1746-1896* (Princeton, 1946), 137.

peers. Classes or study in their rooms filled the time from nine to twelve and again from two to five. Evening prayers at five were followed by supper at six. There was a stretch of free time, then study period from eight to ten, with tutors making the rounds to check attendance and preserve order. At ten, candles and fireplaces (or Franklin stoves) were put out, and the day ended. That was the daily routine which prevailed not only at Princeton but, with slight modifications, on every campus in the land.

Student behavior was secured by a code of laws, of which every undergraduate had a copy. The Code of 1760 of the College of New Jersey, which was similar to those of Yale and Harvard, prescribed attendance at all classes, at prayers twice a day, and at church on Sundays. Playing cards, rolling dice, and frequenting taverns was strictly forbidden. Freshmen had to run errands for upper classmen. Students were required to tip their hats to the president at a distance of ten rods, and to tutors at five. This code, reprinted from time to time, did not vary much over the years. In 1802 and again in 1851, it read much as it had in 1760; the "Laws of 1870" still contained regulations like the following: An exemplary regard to moral and religious duties is indispensable in every officer of the college. . . . All officers have the right to enter the rooms of students at their pleasure. To the tutors is especially committed the preservation of order and decorum. . . . Boisterous noise, keeping horses, blowing horns, kindling bonfires, student meetings without permission of the President, leaving town without permission, are all forbidden.

The regime at Rutgers was similar except for the fact that the faculty, in the absence of dormitories, did not exercise twenty-four-hour control over the student's day. Yet they managed to pre-empt most of his waking hours, as the "Laws of Queen's College" for 1810 clearly show. This was when the college had reopened after a decade of suspension and had moved into the new building on its own campus. A pamphlet of 22 pages, the "Laws" prescribed study and classes from nine to twelve, two to five, and seven to nine in winter, and from five to seven (in the morning), eight to twelve, and three to six in summer. Students had to "orate" in rotation at evening prayers, and public oral examinations were prescribed for the close of each semester, in September and April. Extravagance as well as slovenliness in dress were discountenanced. Students and faculty had to wear the black academic gown in church, at prayers, at examinations, and at public exhibitions. As at Princeton, students were obliged to remove their hats to the president and the professors, though no distances were prescribed. Lower classmen were to yield "modest and respectful deportment" to upper. Students were not permitted to keep dogs, horses, or guns; they were forbidden to take dancing lessons, go to the theater, or to play billiards, cards, or dice "for a wager." They could apparently visit billiard halls and bowling alleys, taverns, beer and oyster houses, upon getting express permission from some officer of the college. Finally, "no student shall employ a barber on the Lord's day to dress his head or shave him nor shall he pay visits on that day or encourage the visits of others, nor shall he spend any part of the day in amusements, recreation or unnecessary secular business."

That adolescents thus cribbed, cabin'd and confined, would resist such rules, was a foregone conclusion. Autocracy tempered by rebellion would be a fair description of the life on most campuses. At Princeton, the early decades of the nineteenth century were a time of well-nigh chronic anarchy. Much of the time, student resistance took the form of crude horseplay and thoughtless destructiveness. A wagon was carried piece by piece to the fourth floor, put together there, and sent rumbling up and down the corridor. Horses were ridden up and down the first floor at midnight. When the food got too bad, knives, forks, plates, and the tablecloth went out the windows. In 1814 "a log filled with two pounds of gunpowder blew open the center door of Nassau Hall, cracked the walls from top to bottom, sent a big splinter through the prayer hall door, and broke windowpanes all over the building." * Some years later, an undergraduate returning to Nassau Hall from an afternoon walk saw the president sitting at the window of his house and, unable to resist the perfect target, pulled out his pistol and took a shot at him. He proved a poor marksman; why he was carrying a pistol was not explained.

Ample powers resided in the college officers to curb such outbreaks, but they were not always wisely used. Though endowed with a high sense of duty, presidents and professors sometimes lacked that subtle understanding of adolescents which marks the successful teacher and school administrator. Scorning all current romantic notions of the innate goodness of man, they based their disciplinary policies on the more easily verifiable doctrine of total human depravity. Some vacillated from one view to the other. John Maclean, associated with the College of New Jersey from 1822 to 1868, as tutor, professor, and finally as president, is described as a vigilant but lenient disciplinarian, generous and easily deceived. He is known to have chased students into their rooms and up trees; he hauled them personally out of taverns. His colleagues on the faculty were capable of meting out severe penalties on hearsay evidence. No clear case was ever made out against the boys who were expelled for setting fire to Nassau Hall. When on another occasion a student was caught ringing the college bell in the middle of the night, the faculty tumbled out of bed at three in the morning and expelled him then and there. Admittedly the provocation was great. In 1807, President Smith and the faculty almost wrecked the college when they broke up an organized rebellion by suspending 125 of a total student body of two hundred. Rutgers, lacking a dormitory, apparently was spared the worst of these mutinous "extra-curricular activities."

* Nathaniel Burt, "Student Life," *Nassau Hall 1756-1956,* Henry Lyttleton Savage, ed. (Princeton, 1956), 128.

Other types of punishment were available to college authorities, less drastic than expulsion. Public admonition was effective with some culprits. Others responded to confinement in their rooms and suspension of privileges. Money fines, though widely used in American colleges at the time, do not seem to have played a large role in the New Jersey institutions. Harvard, by contrast, had had an elaborate system of fines from colonial days on: two pence for tardiness at prayers; three shillings for going fishing without leave or staying away from church services on Sundays; five shillings for fighting, lying, or drunkenness; ten shillings for cursing, playing cards, or firing guns in the Yard. In other colleges, where the practice continued into the nineteenth century, fines might range from two or three cents for cutting class or prayers to two or three dollars for getting ostentatiously drunk or beating up a professor.

Both New Jersey schools, originating as they had in religious revivals, made much of the persuasive powers of religion, publicly in the daily prayer meetings and by appeal to the individual conscience. After all, every president of Princeton down to 1902 was a clergyman, as were most of the presidents of Rutgers and a majority of the professors of both. The religious appeal was not without success. Seasons of revival and evangelical fervor, which periodically swept through the churches of America, had their repercussions on college campuses, and those of New Jersey were no exception. When Ashbel Green, who in his student days at Nassau Hall had considered himself the only professing Christian in the place, became president in 1812, he set out to raise the moral standards of his Alma Mater by a series of religious convocations, sugared with invitations to students to dinner at his home in squads of eight. For a time, behavior improved and many students displayed a new tenderness of conscience. But the inevitable relapse set in, and Green sadly admitted that his policy had but little effect in reclaiming the vicious. A great revival, whose effects were felt for some time, swept Rutgers

College and the city of New Brunswick in 1837, the year of the great Panic and depression. But in general, results were discouraging. The emotional glow induced by evangelical preaching, when not followed up by systematic and purposeful intellectual and social activity, was a straw fire which soon burned out. Students became immune through overexposure and learned to cultivate the art of passive resistance. In this respect New Jersey boys were probably not unlike the student in a New England college in the 1840's, who regularly confided to his diary: "Sunday. Professor X preached. I slept. . . . A day of fasting and prayer for colleges. I neither fasted nor prayed."*

Looking back from mid-twentieth century, we are inclined to ask why the colleges did not introduce a diversified program of extra-curricular activities, which would have enlivened the drab routine and gone a long way toward solving their moral and disciplinary problems. A complete answer would have to take a number of factors into account, but one main reason was the belief that such activities were frivolous distractions which undermined the serious purpose of a college. One exception was permitted, in fact encouraged. That was the literary and debating society. Skill in oratory and debating was held a valuable asset, whether the student was preparing for the ministry, the law, or any other kind of public service. The famous Whig and Cliosophic societies of Princeton date from 1769 and 1770, respectively, and their twin Ionic temples, as rebuilt in the 1890's, still grace the campus. Their Rutgers counterparts, the Peithessophian and the Philoclean—Peitho and Philo—were organized in 1825, the year of the college's revival under its new name. They were the successors of even earlier societies that dated back to colonial times and had enough vitality to survive the fugitive years of the Revolution. Van Nest Hall became their home.

The subjects to which these societies addressed their

* William G. Hammond, *Remembrance of Amherst* (New York, 1946), 231.

attention, whether in their secret weekly meetings or in formal displays at commencement time, ranged broadly if superficially over the whole of human affairs. In dead earnest for the most part, but sometimes with tongue in cheek, the undergraduates would discuss topics like the following: The glaring stupidity of skepticism; The deterioration of the fashions; Is the warrior to be preferred before the philosopher; Ought freedom of thought be granted to all men; Which tends more to relieve a female of celibacy, wealth or a beautiful face. But there were these topics also—for the Queen's debaters in 1787: Should the new Federal Constitution be adopted by the United States; and in Nassau Hall half a century later: Should the abolition of slavery be a condition of admitting states into the Union.

Dramatic performances, too, were part of the permitted extra-curricular activities. They were usually sponsored by the literary societies and were recurrently popular, even though attendance at the public theater was frowned upon. A cryptic bit from the early records of Queen's furnishes a glimpse: "The students of Queen's College solicit the company of Dr. Ryker and Lady at an exhibition of a tragedy on Wednesday the 19th Instant at 6 o'clock in the Evening. . . . Admittance by this card." * The card, turned over, was the eight of clubs. Interest in dramatics at Nassau Hall was sporadic before the days of the Triangle Club, though there was a period soon after the Revolution when sentimental plays were acted regularly, and with such enthusiasm that copious tears were shed in the audience. From time to time the literary societies generated enough intellectual momentum to produce a magazine. These efforts were ephemeral, usually collapsing when the initial fervor cooled or the editors graduated. Articles in student publications, while not ignoring campus problems, took on the coloring of the contemporaneous romantic age. "The Dying Mother," "A Temperance Tale," "A Chris-

* William H. S. Demarest, *A History of Rutgers College 1766-1924* (New Brunswick, 1924), 149.

THE PRINCETON DRAMATIC ASSOCIATION IN 1893

"The Honorable Julius Caesar" was co-authored by Booth Tarkington who, as armed Cassius, is here appropriately next to Caesar.

tian's Last Hour," are examples of titles appearing in the *Rutgers Literary Miscellany* for 1842.

The student literary societies, with their persistent if fumbling search for truth and their Cook's Tour of the issues of the day, were probably the most liberal part of the "liberal" education at Princeton and Rutgers in the nineteenth century. They dealt with live issues, or at any rate with questions that seemed relevant to their members. They acquired libraries, sometimes larger and nearly always broader in scope than the official college library. They filled a social vacuum, were an outlet for joiners, and helped solve problems of discipline. In the opinion of one Princeton alumnus, George Strawbridge, his society did more "to remove boyish habits and make men of us" * than anything else the college had to offer.

The societies had a wholesome effect on standards of scholarship. Their competitive character insured hard work and creditable public performance. An additional incentive were the occasional open meetings, when the general public including young ladies were invited. Before such a "learned, polite, and brilliant assembly," a letter-perfect rendition meant infinitely more than did a perfect translation of Plato or Horace in the presence of nobody but one's bored classmates and the professor who marked the effort for syntax. It was in the debates and oratorical contests that they died for dear old Rutgers in those days. Most important of all, the societies belonged to the students; they initiated the programs and set the standards. A professor might be elected advisor or honorary member, but the management remained with the undergraduates. When, on other campuses, a misguided faculty tried to take over the campus societies, it smothered them. The faculties of Princeton and Rutgers had the good sense to keep their hands off.

Both colleges lacked all provision for systematic physical exercise, which seems almost incredible to us today when organized athletics plays such a prominent role in

* Thomas J. Wertenbaker, *Princeton 1746-1896* (*Princeton,* 1946), 203.

A DELTA UPSILON GROUP AT RUTGERS, IN EARLY 1894

Music and My Lady Nicotine, to say nothing of martial ardor, all had their earnest adherents.

schools at all levels. At that time, to be sure, most organized sports as we know them now had not yet come into existence. But the faculty of Princeton, at least, opposed even those primitive games in which students occasionally indulged as "low and unbecoming gentlemen and students." * Besides, they were considered dangerous to health. Yet some exceptions were made. At Rutgers an outdoor bowling alley was popular from the school's earliest days, apparently with faculty consent. The boys at Nassau Hall satisfied their needs for physical exercise by walking, racing around the perimeter of the campus, rolling hoops in the basement, and playing handball against the president's house, much as young men in the Basque country today play *pelota* against the wall of the village church. Then there were the seasonal sports on both campuses: swimming, skating, sleighing, though the last-named was often forbidden, perhaps because a tavern loomed at the end of the ride.

It was 1850 and later before systematic exercise and organized games became part of the program. The first American college to introduce compulsory training in physical education under a member of the faculty was Amherst, in 1860. Princeton built a gymnasium, a crude barnlike structure, in 1859, at a cost of $984.31, and equipped it with flying rings, trapeze, and parallel bars. It burned down in 1865, and was replaced four years later by a stone structure that looked like a French chateau; in 1902 a "modern" gymnasium was built which was then considered the finest in the country. Rutgers talked about a gymnasium in the 1850's but it did not become an actuality until 1894 when Ballantine Hall was erected, an excellent gymnasium for that day. It burned in 1929 and was replaced by the present gymnasium.

For a number of years in the 1870's gymnastic work of high quality went on in Princeton's second building. Here one of the foremost gymnasts of the country, George Goldie, taught the arts of the horizontal and

* Thomas J. Wertenbaker, *Princeton 1746-1896* (Princeton, 1946), 138.

parallel bars and the flying trapeze. Invited to Princeton from Scotland, he built up a college-wide program of gymnastics and body-building, with the enthusiastic approval of President McCosh. Goldie set such high standards of proficiency, that his best students were compared favorably with the professional gymnasts of the Barnum and Bailey Circus.

Rowing, one of the first competitive collegiate sports, was practiced at both institutions, though under difficult circumstances. Princeton had a six-oared shell on the Delaware and Raritan Canal, where it practiced for the Saratoga Regatta; after several years of participation in the early 1880's the sport was dropped until the dam was built to make Carnegie Lake. With the Raritan at its front door, Rutgers was more fortunately situated, and for a number of years in the 1870's the Rutgers crew held races there with Stevens Institute, Lawrence Scientific School of Harvard, and with Princeton. But a flood swept the boathouse away and the sport was discontinued, not to be resumed until the 1930's. The snaky Raritan with its ebb and flow was not the best place to build winning crews.

In the years just preceding the Civil War baseball became popular on both campuses. The first game between the two was on May 5, 1866. Princeton won, 40-2, but Rutgers was handicapped, according to a Princeton observer, by playing on a strange field and with only eight men. To insure complete teams in the future, Rutgers thereafter chose its baseball squad in the following ingenious fashion. A student board of directors picked the captain, he picked the second man, the two together picked the third, and so on until nine had been chosen. Princeton distinguished itself on the diamond from the start, defeating various town teams from Orange, New Brunswick, Philadelphia, and Brooklyn, and winning the championship of New Jersey.

The athletic event of greatest historical consequence for both institutions was, as everybody knows, the first intercollegiate football game, played at New Brunswick

FOOTBALL IN 1869

The first intercollegiate football game was played between Rutgers and Princeton in 1869, the former winning by six goals to four. Twenty-five men played on each side.
(From the painting by William M. Boyd)

on November 6, 1869. It was a far cry from its modern counterpart, when Tiger meets Scarlet in the opening game of the season. In view of what college football has since become, that encounter back in 1869 was truly from the age of innocence. It was the first of three scheduled between the two teams for that fall, of which only two were played. The scene was College Field, where the present gymnasium stands; a wooden fence surrounded it and served as bleachers for the rooters of both sides. A trainload of Princeton students had come up with the team. William J. Leggett, 1872, was captain of the Rutgers team, and William S. Gummere, 1870, led Princeton's. The latter, as befitted a future chief justice of New Jersey, had drawn up a set of rules which was accepted by Rutgers. There were 25 men on each side. The ball, round and of black rubber, had to be kicked or batted with the fist. Throwing the ball or running with it were not permitted. The team that kicked the ball between the opponents' goal posts at any height—there was no crossbar—scored one point. Thus the game was more like soccer than modern American football. The players wore no uniforms, but took off their hats and coats and fell to. The Rutgers boys wore scarlet turbans, the first use of the college colors on an athletic field. There were no coaches or trainers, apparently no referee, and no choice seats on the fifty-yard-line. A whole row of spectators was bowled over when two players crashed into the fence. The game lasted from three o'clock until dark and ended with Rutgers the winner, 6 to 4.

Afterward, the teams sat down together to a supper of roast game, and the evening was given to post-mortems, impromptu speeches, and college songs. What these were is not recorded. They could have included "Old Nassau," composed in 1859, but not "On the Banks," which dates from 1873. Both songs, by the way, were written in response to particular situations and virtually "on demand." In 1859, Harlan Page Peck, a freshman, wrote a poem, "In Praise of Old Nassau," to be sung to the tune of "Auld Lang Syne." But the tune did not fit the words. At a pipe and beer session of several seniors and tutors the question of a better tune came up. One of the tutors present was Karl Langlotz, son of a German court musician, who had come to America and been appointed instructor in German at the College of New Jersey. An accomplished pianist and violinist, he had also organized various musical groups on campus. One of the party now asked Langlotz to write new music for Peck's poem. He consented, then promptly forgot all about it. Some days later, his friend re-appeared in his room with lined music paper and a pencil, demanding that he redeem his promise. Langlotz wrote the tune then and there, with the other standing over him. Words and music appeared in a collection of Princeton songs published that year.

The Rutgers song was written under even greater pressure. One winter day in 1873 the Glee Club found itself in need of a college song for its opening concert that same night, at Metuchen. At three that afternoon the manager of the Glee Club came to the room of Howard N. Fuller, 1874, and asked him to write one. By five o'clock Fuller had completed the words; the Glue Club promptly fitted them to the melody of a popular song and sang it that night at Metuchen to an enthusiastic audience.

The climax of the academic year camc with commencement and the activities surrounding it. Commencement time was originally late September, at the end of the summer semester which had begun in May. The winter semester ran from November to April. Most of this had been copied from European university schedules. An autumn vacation of six weeks and a spring vacation of four separated the two semesters. But then, to meet American climatic conditions, the academic calendar was changed so as to have one long vacation stretch through the summer, when Princeton and New Brunswick got pretty warm. In 1840, commencement festivities at Nassau Hall were shifted to the last week in June; Rutgers, under the new dispensation after 1825, moved its celebration to the middle of July and, in 1859, to the third week in June. Final examinations of the senior class preceded commencement. As in colleges generally, these were oral and public until about 1850. The faculty conducted the examination, but trustees and other gentlemen with college degrees were privileged to ask questions as well. The seniors resented this procedure, especially the questions from the trustees whom they considered stuffed-shirts. To fail publicly was not pleasant, yet there may have been some perverse satisfaction in going out with a bang instead of a whimper.

In addition to the graduation exercises proper, the festivities usually included a debate or an oratorical contest by the literary societies, the president's reception, alumni reunions that grew bigger and better, and other fringe activities which, in the chaste prose of the historian of Rutgers, "were of not quite academic flavor." The final exercises would get under way at mid-morning with a procession, made up of the student body, the president and faculty, the trustees, the governor of New Jersey and such members of the legislative and judicial branches as could be rounded up, visiting dignitaries, and citizens of the town. Led by the president, or the band, or even the janitor, the assemblage moved to the largest church in town, where all remaining seats were already occupied by parents and friends, and settled down to be edified, as the humidity mounted, by the young gentlemen of the graduating class. Strung along between the salutatorian who welcomed the assembly in Latin and the valedictorian who was either the best scholar or the most important member of the class, each candidate for a degree delivered an oration, or read a poem or an essay, or took part in a disputation. These performances were interspersed with musical selections. At one Rutgers commencement in the 1850's there were 17 speeches and 21 interludes. It was late in the afternoon before such a program was exhausted, along with the audience.

The two college towns meanwhile took on a carnival

aspect, with hucksters in the streets selling confections and gimcracks. Contemporary accounts speak of processions of private carriages, of crowded stagecoaches, crowded boats, and special trains. While the participants at Rutgers were mostly from New Jersey and southern New York, guests at Nassau Hall came from as far away as Virginia. Both towns were on the main road between New York and Philadelphia, and ease of access increased when the Delaware and Raritan Canal was built in 1833 and the railroad the year after. In 1839 the first through-trains ran from New York to Philadelphia, with stops at New Brunswick and Princeton Junction. Though innocent gaiety predominated at commencement time, there were occasional excesses that drew criticism. At one New Brunswick celebration an annoyed observer found the behavior of the young ladies in throwing bouquets most disgraceful, and at another time the police had to be called to quell the crowds competing for seats three hours before the exercises were to begin. Later in the century public participation fell off; other forms of entertainment appeared, and farmers of the surrounding countryside could not come in late June, during the haying season, as they had in late September. From this time forward, the noisy and bibulous part of the celebration was increasingly taken over by nostalgic alumni.

Commencement over, the academic community disbanded. Students scattered to their various homes, all over New Jersey, up the Hudson valley, and into the South and Southwest. The two deserted college towns settled into late summer somnolence, waiting for the first brisk breezes of autumn when the young gentlemen would reassemble at Nassau Hall and Old Queen's for another season of communion with the muses.

IV

THE PARTING OF THE WAYS

DURING THE FIRST HALF of the nineteenth century the College of New Jersey at Princeton, and Rutgers College at New Brunswick, were alike in purpose and character. Both were colleges of liberal arts which, though legally independent, had benefited from their association with the churches that had founded them and from whose domination they were trying to free themselves. The College of New Jersey was the larger, for its Presbyterian constituency was more numerous and widespread than that of the Reformed Church, which centered in New Jersey and New York and looked upon Rutgers as its college. By 1860 the older institution was definitely forging ahead of its younger contemporary both in size and prestige; yet there was every reason to suppose that the two colleges would retain their historic character and develop a relationship within the State of New Jersey not unlike that between Yale and Wesleyan in Connecticut, or Williams and Amherst in Massachusetts. But in 1864 an event occurred which was to turn Rutgers in a new direction. Unforeseen and unintended at the time, a chain of consequences was then set in motion that was to culminate 90 years later in the emergence of Rutgers as the publicly controlled State University of New Jersey. while Princeton was to become one of the most distinguished independent universities of the nation.

The turning point was the enactment of a law by

the New Jersey Legislature in 1864 designating Rutgers as the beneficiary of the Federal Land Grant Act of 1862, commonly known as the Morrill Act. This Act of Congress appropriated the proceeds of the sale of land in the public domain for the purpose of furthering higher education. Each state was entitled to thirty thousand acres for each senator and representative in Congress. States like New Jersey, which had no public domain within its borders, could lay claim to an equivalent amount in the west where there was acreage to spare. The money derived from the sale of the land could be used to found a new institution of higher learning or to support the appropriate courses in an existing one; the conditions were that the college created or designated by the state must offer courses in agriculture and the mechanic arts, whatever else it taught, and that it must provide military training, for the legislation was enacted in the midst of the Civil War.

There seems to have been no sentiment for a new college in New Jersey, for it was a small state and already had two colleges. But neither was it self-evident that Rutgers would receive the grant rather than Princeton. Both institutions were doing respectable work in the sciences as such work was measured in those days; both were receptive to any offer from the State, in token of which each was about to set up a separate scientific school. It may be that Rutgers, a little more emancipated from church control, was for that reason considered more entitled to public funds. After all, Rutgers had had lay presidents since 1840, a radical departure at a time when nine-tenths of all college presidents were clergymen. One of these layman-presidents, Theodore Frelinghuysen, was easily the most prominent national figure to hold the presidential office at either Rutgers or Princeton in the nineteenth century. A graduate of Princeton himself, Frelinghuysen was the son of General Frederick Frelinghuysen of Revolutionary War fame, who in turn had been the first tutor of Queen's College. He was United States Senator from New Jersey and is best known to history as vice-presidential candidate on the Whig ticket with Henry Clay in the election of 1844. Belonging to the "Conscience Whig" faction of the party, as opposed to the "Cotton Whigs," he was active in reform movements, a leader in the campaign for public schools in New Jersey—as was President Maclean of Princeton—and one-time head of the American Temperance Society, the American Tract Society, and similar organizations. Coming to Rutgers from the chancellorship of New York University, he was president from 1850 until his death in 1862.

The claims of Rutgers to the land-grant funds were ably supported by prominent alumni. These included Frederick T. Frelinghuysen, brother of Theodore, also a United States Senator and later Secretary of State in the cabinet of President Arthur; Joseph P. Bradley, soon to be elevated to the United States Supreme Court; and Cortlandt Parker, President of the American Bar Association. But the man who really turned the scales in favor of Rutgers, and at the same time prepared the college educationally to make significant use of the grant, was George H. Cook. A professor of chemistry, Cook was a native of New Jersey and a graduate of Rensselaer Polytechnic Institute. He came to Rutgers in 1853. His scientific interests were broad: he became state geologist, organized a meteorological service, and promoted scientific agriculture. He also initiated what has since become the broad field of agricultural extension services. To have such a man associated with the college in New Brunswick weighed heavily in its favor. It was in March, 1864, that the Legislature voted, twelve to six in the Senate, fifty to one in the Assembly, to designate the trustees of Rutgers College as the recipients of the land-grant monies for use in the newly constituted Rutgers Scientific School. It amounted to $5800 a year, interest at five percent on the $116,000 which New Jersey had received from the sale of the public lands allotted to the State.

The selection of Rutgers as the land-grant college of

New Jersey did not automatically make it the State University. The action of the Legislature was not irreversible. The arrangement with the State could easily have been terminated at any time within the next thirty years or before the latter began to make direct appropriations for buildings and equipment, and perhaps even after that had both principals so desired. This happened in other states; the Morrill appropriation in Connecticut first went to Sheffield Scientific School of Yale, in Massachusetts to Massachusetts Institute of Technology, in New Hampshire to Dartmouth. In all three instances it was later transferred to the new agricultural colleges in each of those states, which in turn became the state universities. New Jersey followed the unique course of gradually converting an existing private college into its state university.

For the first twenty-five years the new program did not amount to much. Fifty-eight hundred dollars a year was little enough to go on, even in those days of low prices; besides, it cost the Rutgers trustees thirty thousand dollars to buy and equip the experimental "College Farm." The course of study of the scientific school was set at three years, and increased to four in 1870. The Princeton school of science, when first proposed in 1864, was also to be a three-year program. The main divisions of the Rutgers school were agriculture, engineering, and chemistry. Students completing the course would receive the Bachelor of Science degree instead of the traditional Bachelor of Arts degree. Admission requirements waived the whole classical-philosophical apparatus and included only arithmetic, algebra, English grammar, and geography. Under the direction of Professor Cook three new faculty members were added, one for agriculture, one for chemistry and metallurgy, and one for engineering and military science. The first class numbered 13, all of whom came to study engineering. This disproportion held for the classes that followed, and the agricultural college was really an engineering school until the end of the century.

Yet for all the efforts of Professor Cook and his colleagues, the new school lacked prestige. In this, New Jersey was not unique; the land-grant agricultural colleges everywhere, and especially in the eastern states, were slow to gain recognition. Their low entrance requirements provoked widespread criticism, and the intrenched classical colleges looked down on them as second-class academic citizens. In his memoirs of college days, a Yale graduate of the 1880's recalled that in the opinion of himself and his classmates, "Sheff [Sheffield Scientific School] did not count."*

Meantime, agricultural programs were being expanded by the establishment of agricultural experiment stations. The New Jersey (State) Agricultural Experiment Station was established in 1880, and located by its board of managers on the Rutgers "College Farm." In 1887, Congress established agricultural experiment stations at the several land-grant colleges, including of course Rutgers. The two stations were maintained as distinct entities for many years, but were operationally integrated. In 1889, the State provided a building, New Jersey Hall, on the Rutgers campus. The next year Congress implemented the Morrill Act by voting direct annual funds to land-grant colleges, and in the same year New Jersey made its first direct financial subsidy to Rutgers in the form of tuition scholarships. The legality of the latter was promptly contested. Litigation ensued, and for the next 14 years Rutgers absorbed the cost of the scholarships, accepting the State students whose tuition the State refused to pay. Finally, in 1904, the highest State court, following the recommendation of a commission of inquiry, upheld the right of Rutgers to the money, and the State paid eighty thousand dollars in accumulated tuition fees.

As the turn of the century drew near, rapprochement of State and college continued, though at an uneven pace. The college's own building program was influenced by the new direction. Geological Hall, built in 1872—the

* Robert N. Corwin, *The Plain Unpolished Tale of the Workaday Doings of Modest Folk* (New Haven, 1948), 76.

first new building in almost thirty years—contained science lecture rooms and laboratories on the main floor, a notable natural science museum on the top floor, and the armory of the military department in the basement. Then a chemistry building and an engineering building, both erected with private funds, were equipped by the State. A little later the State authorized instruction and research in ceramics—a reflection of New Jersey's clay deposits and the importance of its pottery industry—and eventually erected a building for this division. Soon after, short courses in agriculture were instituted, supported by public funds. State ties were strengthened still further when, in 1918, a women's college was established under the Rutgers Charter, amid pointed references to the obligation of a land-grant college to provide higher education for women as well as for men. This new institution, significantly named New Jersey College for Women, almost immediately requested—and received—legislative appropriations for buildings and maintenance. It was in the early twentieth century, too, that the last vestigial remains of denominational affiliation were removed. Charter amendment and supplementary action abolished the requirement that the president and a fixed percentage of the trustees must be members of the Reformed Church. With these final restrictions gone, the college was fully independent of church control and influence.

State support for a part of the Rutgers program led to no diminution of efforts on its behalf by the historic private constituency of the college. On the contrary, these increased. The alumni individually and collectively began to play a constantly larger role in promoting the welfare of their Alma Mater, and gifts of all kinds grew in size and frequency. For the Centennial celebration in 1870—at that time no one knew of the existence of the first charter in 1766—the alumni pledged one hundred forty thousand dollars. Geological Hall was built with some of these funds. Other buildings followed, their names commemorating their donors: Kirkpatrick Chapel,

Ballantine Gymnasium, Voorhees Library. The chapel soon began to acquire that remarkable collection of portraits of Rutgers worthies which crowds its walls today and exercises a strange influence on the visitor in the pew. From Jacob Hardenbergh, prominent up front, to the latest president or trustee above the rear pews, these makers of Rutgers and New Jersey history gaze down on the worshiper and fill him with such an overwhelming sense of the past as to blot out all awareness of the program and speaker of the moment. Culmination of the alumni effort in this phase of Rutgers history was a successful million-dollar endowment campaign at the close of the second decade of the century.

When the Sesquicentennial date rolled around, in 1916 —the right year this time—Rutgers could look back on a century and a half of growth and achievement. Yet it was still a small college with a narrow constituency and limited influence. It was no university. Its student enrollment, after fluctuating between two and three hundred for many years, had risen to about five hundred. Tuition was one hundred dollars a year. Creditable work on the undergraduate level was being done in limited fields. Graduate work was in its infancy. The policy of the college, as stated by President William H. S. Demarest— the only alumnus, incidentally, ever to have become president of Rutgers—could be paraphrased about as follows: Rutgers must build on the historic foundations of Old Queen's. The obligations to the State under the contractual relations of the land-grant act must be clearly recognized and faithfully carried out. Yet this must in no way interfere with the primary emphasis on the college's classical origin, its cultural mission, and its duty to its historic constituency.

Before recounting the final steps of the evolution of Rutgers into the State University, we must go back to the other New Jersey college and trace the story of its astonishing development. By the middle of the nineteenth century the College of New Jersey at Princeton was one of the better known institutions of the country. Conservative in cast, it continued to influence and to draw students from the Presbyterian communities of the middle-Atlantic states, the South and the Southwest, as well as from the dominant, if non-Presbyterian, planter class. It had furnished many presidents and professors to the newer colleges of the interior. But it had not yet attained the prominence in American higher education that it holds today. It was not mentioned in the same breath with Harvard and Yale, nor did it share with them the leadership of any nineteenth-century equivalent of the Ivy League.

The Civil War brought reverses and temporary shrinkage in size and prestige. Because of its well-known Southern connections, the trustees and faculty of Nassau Hall were at some pains after Fort Sumter to disavow any sympathy with secession and to protest their loyalty to the Union. Student enrollment dropped from 314 to 221 in 1861-1862, and continued to decline as students gave up their studies to enlist in the armed forces. This was true, of course, of Rutgers and of American colleges generally, but Princeton probably had more students and alumni in both Union and Confederate armies than any other college. The students from the South never came back. Yet even without them, the conservative and mildly pro-Southern character of college and town lingered on. When Lucy Stone, feminist and abolitionist, came to Princeton with her husband a year after Appomattox to plead the cause of Negro suffrage and women's rights, the meeting was broken up "by boys and young men said to be students of the College of New Jersey." The local newspaper commented: "We regret the disgraceful blackguardism at Mercer Hall . . . though such a population as that of Princeton could not be supposed to countenance the propriety of woman appearing on the rostrum to advocate political rights."*

In the postwar decade Princeton was smaller and in

* Herbert McAneny, "Some Notes on Princeton Amusements, Civil War to 1887," *The Princeton University Library Chronicle* (November, 1942).

some ways more provincial than before the war. In these years the percentage of students enrolling from New Jersey was probably larger than at any time before or since. The total enrollment in 1868, the last year of the Maclean regime, was only 281. As late as 1886, the college failed to receive any particular recognition at the two-hundred-fiftieth anniversary celebration at Harvard. Of 42 honorary degrees awarded on that occasion to distinguished scholars in many fields, not one went to a Princeton man; and the "Commemoration Ode" by Oliver Wendell Holmes, whose vision was pretty well limited to New England, listed Yale, Amherst, Williams, and Bowdoin, before it condescendingly admitted Princeton to the circle. But by that time events were stirring in Nassau Hall which would within a few years make a repetition of such a slight unthinkable.

In 1868 the College of New Jersey once again turned to Scotland for leadership, as it had a hundred years earlier, and with equal success. The new president was the Reverend James McCosh, Professor of Logic and Metaphysics at Queen's College, Belfast, a scholar of recognized stature and wide acquaintance in European universities. When McCosh arrived to take office he found a small, sluggish classical college whose faculty and board of trustees were "full of hidebound conservatives." * When he retired twenty years later, the campus had expanded from twenty to seventy acres and had acquired a multitude of new buildings; the student body had doubled in size and grown more mature; the faculty had more than trebled; the library increased five-fold. More remarkably, salaries had advanced from $2100 to $3000 at a time when the cost of living was holding steady if not actually declining. The influence of the college once again extended far beyond the borders of New Jersey, for McCosh, like his eighteenth-century Scottish predecessor, went to the Nation in long and frequent journeys to present his cause. One such

* Thomas J. Wertenbaker, *Princeton 1746-1896* (Princeton, 1946), 309.

trip alone included stops at Washington, Detroit, Cincinnati, St. Louis, Chicago, Frankfort and Lexington, Kentucky. In all externals, a most successful administration; its gains in scholarship will be reviewed in the next chapter.

The stirring days of McCosh were followed by a decade and a half of more quiet growth and assimilation, during which, however, the enrollment doubled once again, passing the twelve-hundred mark soon after 1900. Then came the eight stormy years under Woodrow Wilson, full of brilliant innovation and bitter controversy—as well as constant headlines. When Wilson left to become Governor of New Jersey, in 1910, no institution of higher learning in the United States was more widely known than Princeton.

How shall one account for this feat? Unexpected changes in direction and pace in the affairs of men and institutions are among the puzzles of history. Though the techniques of the social scientists are constantly enlarging the areas of established fact, they have not thus far succeeded in isolating or eliminating the unpredictable and imponderable, that which we call the unique element in human personality and the unquenchable spirit of man. Why did Princeton, starting equal with a score or more of other independent colleges, outdistance them all? Why did Rutgers, from a similar start, move into the orbit of the State? In retrospect one can pick out several circumstances that offer a partial explanation only. One can point out, for example, that the last third of the nineteenth century saw Princeton acquiring, in addition to McCosh and Wilson, an unusual number of competent scholars and successful and concerned trustees. But this only leads to the next question: why was Princeton able to gather such men to a degree that others did not, and where did they come from? In large part they came from the Presbyterian Church, which was rapidly growing in wealth and prominence throughout the nation, and from the alumni, of whom the same can be said. In many cases the two sources were the same. There were other Presbyterian colleges, but none had the age or the record of participation in the nation's history that Nassau Hall could boast. Thus Princeton, in a sense, raised itself by its own bootstraps. Rutgers, by contrast, could draw on no such reservoir of wealth and manpower, for though the Reformed Church and the Dutch citizenry also produced their share of successful and brilliant men, these were much fewer in number and confined to a smaller geographic area.

Actual tutelage to the church, to be sure, had by this time been shaken off. If proof were needed, it came through an incident at the end of the century, when Presbyterian authorities complained about the college's alleged tolerance toward students' drinking in the taverns of the town. In reply, President Patton, himself a Presbyterian minister, insisted that the faculty were dealing responsibly and intelligently with the problem, and added: "I will do what in me lies to keep the hand of ecclesiasticism from resting on Princeton University." * In spite of this declaration of independence, Princeton continued to receive increasing support from well-to-do Presbyterian laymen and influential Presbyterian clergymen, all usually alumni.

Whatever the reason for this unprecedented expansion, it was a fact, and the expansion soon increased its rate of speed. The alumni now began that continuous and systematic support which they still provide and which has made Princeton, along with Dartmouth, the foremost educational institution of the country in percentage of its alumni who contribute funds. In recognition of their increasing assistance the alumni were finally, after years of agitation, given permanent representation on the board of trustees, a position from which they gained further leverage. Donations multiplied, and instead of thousands of dollars, the college gradually accustomed itself to think in terms of millions. Three millions,

* Thomas J. Wertenbaker, *Princeton 1746-1896* (Princeton, 1946), 375.

in gifts of all kinds, came in during the twenty years of the McCosh administration; the gifts continued to flow during the next regime; and Woodrow Wilson in his first annual report to the trustees in 1902, asked for six million dollars for immediate needs—six million although the college apparently could not yet afford a full-time secretary for the president, who wrote all his letters in his own hand or with part-time student help.

Immediate tangible results came in the form of new buildings. Beginning in the late 1860's, a building program was launched which transformed the campus and whose momentum has continued with few interruptions to the present day. A gymnasium, the octagonal library, and a school of science building initiated the program and before the end of the McCosh administration several large dormitories and the Marquand Chapel had been added.

All these changes came into public notice at the elaborate Sesquicentennial celebration of 1896, which had been in preparation for three years and which furnished the occasion for the official change of the hundred-and-fifty-year-old college to Princeton University. Both President McCosh and Patton, as well as many others concerned, had been urging this step for years, but the trustees hung back, fearful of entering upon the unknown and giving up the tested and tried. True, Princeton was not a full university in the historic European sense: it had no schools of medicine or law, only indirect access to a school of theology, and its graduate program was rudimentary. But it did have schools of science and engineering and programs in the fine arts, all of which marked a long advance over the narrow classical curriculum of thirty years earlier. And so the change was made. At the last climactic meeting of the Sesquicentennial, which featured a speech by United States President Grover Cleveland on the need for college graduates in the public service, President Patton announced that "from this moment what heretofore for one hundred and fifty years has been known as the

College of New Jersey shall in all future time be known as Princeton University." *

Rutgers was to wait nearly thirty years, until 1924, before it too was officially called a university, and when the change of title did come, it marked another forward step in Rutgers' association with the State.

* Thomas J. Wertenbaker, *Princeton, 1746-1896* (Princeton, 1946), 373.

V

FROM COLLEGE TO UNIVERSITY

THE CHANGE FROM COLLEGE to university meant more than an official alteration of title. To understand its full implications one must go back to the beginning of higher education in America. When Harvard, William and Mary, and Yale were founded, they were set up as copies of similar colleges in the university towns of Cambridge and Oxford. Unlike their English prototypes, however, they did not become the first units of a succession of such colleges which collectively formed a university, but through force of circumstances rather than by design each remained a single independent college instead of becoming part of a larger whole. This pattern was followed by all the others, including Princeton and Rutgers. Though some of them—Harvard, for example—early assumed the name of university, they were all in fact four-year undergraduate institutions offering the limited and, on the whole, non-professional course of study which we have described. This was the American college, different from anything in Europe. But when, late in the nineteenth century, the centrifugal forces which had molded American life up to that time began to weaken and eventually to reverse direction, the common heritage of Western civilization was rediscovered, and with it the university. Three factors were of primary importance in this change of direction: first, the establishment of state-owned and tax-supported institutions of higher learning, especially in the Midwest; then, the impact of the philosophy of evolution; and finally, the vogue of German scholarship. The first was an indigenous growth, but the other two came from Europe.

The state university is almost as old, in name at least, as the private college. The University of North Carolina in Chapel Hill was receiving students in 1795, and South Carolina and Georgia followed soon after. Yet these early state schools differed little from the private colleges of that day. A new departure was represented by Thomas Jefferson's University of Virginia with its separate schools and other unconventional devices which made it a distinguished pioneer in the state university movement. But the strongest impetus came after the middle of the nineteenth century from the "Valley of Democracy" west of the Appalachians, with the University of Michigan the prototype. While private colleges flourished there too, public opinion in the Mississippi Valley tended to support institutions owned and supported by the whole state, free from competitive local pride and sectarian strife, as the most flexible and suitable instruments for realizing the educational goals of a democratic society. In such a school not only the classical student laying the foundations for the ministry or the law, but the farmer, the merchant, the mechanic —in short the people—could find the kind of training and information they needed. Here women as well as men would be welcome. It was this democratic groundswell that produced the Morrill Act. Since New Jersey's share of benefits under this law went to Rutgers, the college was destined to reach university status as a state university with its ever-widening departments and vocational schools.

While the state university was broadening the scope of higher education, there was in the making an intellectual revolution of the first magnitude which was to change its fundamental character. The surge of scientific research and philosophical speculation which characterized nineteenth-century Europe was beginning to affect America and to call for recognition and appraisal. Most startling of the new ideas was the theory of evolution. Cautiously advanced by Charles Darwin in his *Origin of Species* in 1859, the theory was expanded into a universal philosophy by Herbert Spencer and carried directly to the lecture-loving and magazine-reading American public by eloquent popularizers; its influence spread contagiously over campus after campus and was soon all-pervasive. Though bitterly opposed by theological and academic conservatives, the theory wormed its way into the laboratories, thus providing the sciences with a firm rationale and raising their professors to the position of pre-eminence in the academic hierarchy once held by the classicists. It offered a fresh point of view in other fields as well and called for a re-examination of accepted methods and values throughout the curriculum. By introducing the organic approach to history and literature it revolutionized the teaching of those subjects, and it speeded the emergence of the social sciences as a separate division of teaching and research. All in all, the evolutionary point of view hastened the expansion of colleges into universities.

While the state university and the theory of evolution broadened the curriculum by multiplying courses and subjects, the third force, German scholarship, gave it depth. For a variety of reasons, German universities had enjoyed an intellectual renaissance in the eighteenth century and, by the close of the Napoleonic era, were coming to be recognized as the best in Europe. It was to German universities that serious American students turned for answers to the new and disturbing intellectual questions of their age. The migration began in a small way after 1815, and increased from a trickle to a steady stream in the decades following the creation of the German Empire by Bismarck in 1871. It is estimated that in the century from 1815 to 1915 nearly ten thousand American scholars studied in Germany. Some adhered to the traditional Latin and Greek studies, some entered the more fashionable field of comparative literature, still others investigated the new research techniques in history, or the new laboratory methods in chemistry, or took up such avant-garde subjects as psychology and cultural anthropology. About all of these subjects and methods, old and new, the German universities had the latest word. What impressed the Americans above all in their foreign venture was the freedom of these universities—freedom of expression for the professor, freedom of choice for the student. It was all so different from the tight lockstep of requirements and regulations of their colleges back home. Equipped with the coveted Doctor of Philosophy degree, open sesame to virtually any academic Chair in the United States, the returning scholars introduced the formal lecture, the laboratory, and the seminar to American campuses, hoping by these refined techniques to raise them to a more mature level.

A new type of intellectual experience was now in store for American undergraduates, and it was provided by a new type of professor: the specialist. The classically trained, clerically oriented teacher who was wont to take on, with equal fortitude, freshman mathematics, sophomore Greek, or senior metaphysics, was gradually replaced by the expert who knew one field thoroughly and built his courses and his reputation on that. The eloquent orator in literature and history was giving way to the methodical lecturer who was grounded in the sources and knew his way among the documents. Dramatic lecturers, to be sure, would continue to flourish, but henceforth their soaring passages would be anchored by footnotes. As for laboratories, they were now forthcoming. A large part of the wealth that legislatures and philanthropic businessmen were beginning to lavish on their universities was being channeled, if not necessary for gymnasiums and stadiums, into the science departments. From Harvard to Stanford, from Minnesota to Texas, the sciences were being supported in a manner to which they had not been accustomed, while the dingy old "philosophical cabinets" and the hit-or-miss demonstrations of the professor of natural philosophy vanished into the Paleozoic past.

Yet the American university which emerged from the efforts of the new-style professors was not an exact replica of the German. In the United States, the new forms of scholarly activity had to be carried on in the existing colleges of liberal arts, or in some kind of extension of those colleges. In the state universities it had to find a place, somehow, among or above the various vocational departments and schools. The German university was not burdened with such encumbrances, since all general education in the liberal arts had been completed in the secondary school, their *Gymnasium,* and the university could devote its entire resources to specialization and research. The American answer to the problem was the graduate school, grafted onto the undergraduate college and providing facilities for the training in research that would lead to advanced degrees. Thus the university, as opposed to the college, represented an expansion vertically as well as horizontally. The American university was an assortment of vocational departments and schools grouped around the core of the original liberal arts college, plus a graduate school of arts and sciences the principal function of which, along with the professional schools on the same advanced level, was systematic scientific research.

As American colleges moved into the enlarged situation, it soon became apparent that the required course of study would have to be overhauled, for the undergraduate could no longer carry the whole load. There were not enough hours in the day for even the flimsiest survey of all the new subjects crowding the curriculum, and yet according to traditional theory and practice, all subjects were required. Something had to give. What was it to be? The answer came from Harvard. In 1869, one year after President McCosh entered office at Princeton and five years after Rutgers had been declared the land-grant college of New Jersey, America's oldest institution of higher learning inaugurated one of its greatest presidents: Charles W. Eliot. This educational statesman cut the Gordian knot of the indigestible curriculum by abolishing required courses altogether and permitting students to choose their own program of study. Having a faculty to contend with, Eliot could not accomplish this reform immediately, but he kept at it and after about twenty years he had achieved his purpose. By 1886 a student could graduate from Harvard upon completing 18 courses, one of which must be freshman English, while the other 17 could be freely chosen in any sequence or combination from among the courses offered in the catalogue.

Elective studies were not altogether unknown on American campuses, though the weight of tradition was against them. The University of Virginia had struck out boldly in that direction forty years before Harvard, and here and there an isolated college—Union, Brown, the University of Nashville—had flirted with this dangerous doctrine. But the Harvard proposals were radical, for they shattered the consensus of centuries that a certain body of knowledge, together with a certain kind of mental discipline, both derived largely from the Greek and Latin classics, marked the educated man. Eliot's reforms implied that there was no such sacred body of subject-matter which could claim priority over all others, but that any organized intellectual activity was worth the student's while. This was exactly what he meant, this was the note he struck in the opening sentence of his inaugural address: "The endless controversies whether language, philosophy, mathematics or science supplies the best mental training . . . have no practical lessons for us today. . . . We would have them all, and at their best." And on another occasion: "The vulgar argument that the study of the classics is necessary to make a gentleman is beyond contempt." * So, in word and action Eliot and Harvard flung down the challenge to the vested interests of the conservative Ameri-

* Henry James, *Charles W. Eliot* (Boston, 1930), I, 196.

can college world. And conservative it was, astonishing as this may seem in a society that was changing more rapidly than any other on the face of the earth. "As stagnant as a Spanish convent" was the verdict of Andrew Dickson White, first president of Cornell, on the older Eastern colleges. There, under the elms, tradition ruled. While Harvard was setting higher education by its ears, many a venerable campus rumbled on undisturbed, as though nothing of importance had happened since Caesar found all Gaul divided into three parts.

The two New Jersey colleges held with the conservative majority. Though not stagnant, as White charged, Princeton and Rutgers chose the path of tradition and took their stand with Yale, chief advocate of the old ways, in setting their faces firmly against the Harvard heresy. President McCosh, though a progressive leader in other ways, gained national acclaim when he challenged Eliot and publicly debated the elective system with him. With rhetorical fervor he proclaimed the eternal values of the traditional curriculum and ridiculed as "mental monstrosities" the students currently turned out at Harvard, who dabbled in music, art, and French plays.* Public opinion in the wake of the debate favored McCosh.

Yet in practice the President was far from being a hidebound reactionary. In spite of the position McCosh had taken in the Eliot debate, he had introduced electives, cautiously and piecemeal, into the junior and senior years. Denounced by the traditionalists in his constituency for such a radical innovation, he was criticized before the end of his administration for not carrying the change far enough.

About evolution, the other great challenge of the day, McCosh was open-minded. Rather than suppress all discussion of the theory, which would only antagonize the students and lead to clandestine reading of Darwin and Huxley, he insisted that the evidence must

* Thomas J. Wertenbaker, *Princeton 1746-1896* (Princeton, 1946), 306.

be faced honestly and accepted if scientifically convincing. Like many other liberal theologians of his day, McCosh interpreted the Darwinian and Spencerian thesis as consistent with theism and a teleological philosophy, and as demonstrating moral progress in the world. "I have been defending Evolution but, in doing so, have given the proper account of it as a method of God's procedure." And again: "We are not be precluded from seeking and discovering a final cause, because we have found an efficient cause."* He took great satisfaction in winning tough-minded students over to a position of religious and ethical commitment, and he liked to cite the case of one undergraduate, an "open-mouthed infidel, perpetually quoting Huxley and Spencer," who ended up lecturing for the Y.M.C.A. In his stand on evolution, McCosh was ahead of the theological position of his church, at any rate as this was reflected in Princeton Theological Seminary. There the leader of opinion was the revered Charles Hodge, Biblical scholar and determined foe of evolution who uncompromisingly insisted that Darwinism was atheism, and who expressed his great satisfaction at the celebration of his semi-centennial in office, that in all his fifty years not a single new idea had come out of Princeton.

The measured pace of progress set by McCosh was not maintained by his immediate successor, but the place fairly crackled with ideas and projects when Woodrow Wilson took over, in 1902. For the next eight years, Princeton was the most talked-about university in the country and reached a position high in America's intellectual hierarchy. It now became a national institution. The growing contacts of Princeton and its President with the world beyond the campus are reflected in Wilson's calendar of speaking engagements. From November, 1905, to February, 1906, for example, he spoke at Orange, New Jersey (on Princeton's future); at Providence, Rhode Island; at Carnegie Hall (on politics); at

* James McCosh, *Christianity and Positivism* (New York, 1875), 8; "Twenty Years at Princeton College" (Farewell Address, 1888).

Hartford, Connecticut; at the Waldorf-Astoria; at a commemoration service for the late President Harper of the University of Chicago; at Charleston, South Carolina (on Americanism); at Brooklyn; and at the Lotos Club in New York City, where he was mentioned for the first time as a possible president of the United States.

The first president of Princeton who was not a Presbyterian minister, Wilson had been elected unanimously by the trustees who did not bother even to consider any other candidate, and with the enthusiastic support of his faculty. His frame of reference was national. He entitled his Inaugural Address, "Princeton in the Nation's Service." Not service to the church alone, or the alumni, or New Jersey, but the Nation. And its chief concern, like that of any university, was intellectual activity. The university was not a social club, its purpose was not to prepare for a job or promote life adjustment, but to discover and teach the disinterested truths of science, literature, and philosophy. Whatever contributed to this end he supported, whatever interfered he opposed, with all the acumen of a trained scholar and all the fervor of a stubborn idealist.

To promote intellectual life among the undergraduates, Wilson introduced a system of small group discussions under the leadership of a member of the faculty. Antedating Harvard's tutorial plan, the preceptorial system, which still distinguishes Princeton, is usually held to be Wilson's most successful contribution not only to his University but to American higher education in general. Fifty preceptors, carefully selected for their scholarly promise and personal qualities, were to meet the students in small groups to guide and stimulate their thinking in such a way as to transform the routine of class lectures and recitations into an adventure of the mind. Another principal achievement was a major reorganization of the curriculum. Here, avoiding both the Scylla of an overcrowded program of required courses and the Charybdis of unpatterned free electives, Wilson and his faculty introduced an arrangement that was to be widely adapted by universities everywhere, and which will be recognized by most graduates today as the system under which they studied. Under this plan, the freshman and sophomore years were largely given over to a sequence of required courses of a general nature in the arts and sciences, while the junior and senior years were built around a single subject, or major, for concentrated advanced work, plus such free electives as the student could fit in. To facilitate orderly choice, the course offerings were organized under twelve departments in four grand divisions: philosophy, art and architecture, language and literature, mathematics and science. Princeton was not the first to introduce this plan of distribution and concentration—as Harvard was to label it when adopting it ten years later—nor did Wilson invent it. Stanford, under President David Starr Jordan, was the first major university to operate under such a plan, and Wilson may well have known of it; again, he may have remembered his early teaching days at Bryn Mawr, where President M. Carey Thomas had already introduced such a program before anyone else.

Not all of Wilson's plans were realized. He suffered a major defeat in the conflict over the graduate school, that other component of a true university. Here Wilson, adhering to his principle of centralized control, came into conflict with another fine scholar and able administrator, Andrew F. West, Professor of Classics, who had been made dean of graduate work and given wide discretionary powers. Dean West's plan, which Wilson had originally endorsed, called for a graduate school whose first concerns would be an outstanding faculty and generous fellowships to attract able students. But it also called for a building complex of its own, away from the main campus, and put control of the whole enterprise in the hands of the dean. Wilson delayed action in favor of his own reform program in the undergraduate college. But the issue was joined when William C. Procter offered five hundred thousand dollars for the graduate school on condition that the school be organized according to

Dean West's plan and controlled by him. Now Wilson had to take a stand. He urged refusal of the gift because in his view it took control of the University out of the hands of the trustees and the president, and he threatened to resign if the money was accepted. In characteristic Wilsonian fashion, he elevated the power struggle into an epic conflict between the forces of democracy and privilege. At this point, Procter withdrew the offer, leaving the president momentarily victorious. But the conflict had left scars; while the majority of the faculty supported Wilson, West had his influential friends too, and a number of trustees had lost confidence in the President.

A month later, the issue was settled when a gift from another source, estimated at between two and three million dollars, was offered as endowment of the graduate school, again provided the West plan be adopted and he remain in charge. At the same time the Procter offer was renewed. The pressure of these millions could no longer be resisted, and Wilson recommended acceptance on the donors' terms. This was in June, 1910. The following autumn he resigned the presidency and was elected Governor of New Jersey.

At Rutgers, as at Princeton, the forces of change were at work, but they operated more slowly and produced no spectacular leader to create controversy and bring them to national attention. The required standard course of study was not officially discarded, but was gradually eroded as new subjects were added and students enrolled for these at the expense of the traditional classical course. Increasingly, toward the end of the nineteenth century, Bachelors of Science in the graduating classes outnumbered the conventional Bachelors of Arts. To stem this tide, admission and course requirements for science students were increased. Finally, in 1916, the faculty reorganized the curriculum and introduced a version of the distribution-concentration system, with required courses in the lower years, majors, minors, and electives in the upper.

Intellectual growth proceeded in other ways. The library, which had been housed in the chapel, received a building of its own in 1903. The forty-six thousand volumes which were moved there in that year included several unusual special collections, but lacked the breadth and depth of a true university library. Long before this event, the new type of academician, the specialist, had begun to infiltrate the faculty and to replace the clergyman-scholar of an earlier day. There had always been good teaching at Rutgers, but it was spotty and uneven. Jacob Cooper, Professor of Greek from 1866 on, was the first Rutgers professor with a German doctoral degree: Berlin, 1854. Soon there were others. Among those who added stature to the college as a place of reputable scholarship Austin Scott stands out, a Yale graduate with a doctorate from Leipzig. Beginning in 1883, Scott served Rutgers for 40 years, first as a professor of history and constitutional law, then for 15 years as president, and then again at his own request as faculty member. His seminar in American Constitutional History, which he had first developed at Johns Hopkins, was a pioneering venture, widely and justly renowned for its originality and high quality. Even before Scott's day, Rutgers had been chosen for membership in Phi Beta Kappa as the Alpha Chapter of New Jersey, the first in the State. The office of dean was created in 1901 and deans soon began to proliferate, a sure sign that the unity of the single-minded classical college was disintegrating. The dean of the college was soon followed by a dean of engineering and one of agriculture. Graduate work was talked about from 1880 on, but students were few and no real organization was achieved until later.

What hastened the transformation of Rutgers into a university was, more than anything else, the scientific school and land-grant college, which began to flourish in the first decade of the twentieth century and through its increasing service to, and support from the State, to gain wide attention. A few examples will illustrate the trend. When in 1882 the States of New York and

New Jersey appointed a joint commission to re-survey their common boundary, three members of the Rutgers faculty participated: one as a member of the commission for New Jersey, one as secretary to the joint commission, and one as director of the actual survey. All three were from the scientific school. Students and graduates of the school helped with the field work. It was in the land-grant college that formal research, an essential feature of a university, was first begun, and from it came the main pressure for acceptance of the evolutionary hypothesis. Professors in their laboratories could hardly do otherwise. The opposition gradually weakened. *Targum,* the undergraduate newspaper, might run an occasional article, possibly faculty-inspired, denouncing the follies of evolution, but these grew fewer. The president meanwhile, like the presidents of most colleges, had the two-fold task of encouraging his science faculty so as to maintain academic standards, while at the same time reassuring the parents of students and the public in general that the college still cherished the eternal values and had no intention of undermining anybody's faith. But the triumph of science was a foregone conclusion, and it enhanced the prestige of the theorists and practitioners of science in the land-grant college.

As the two New Jersey institutions slowly metamorphosed—to paraphrase Herbert Spencer's famous definition of evolution—from indefinite, homogeneous colleges into definite, heterogenous universities, campus life underwent a comparable change and new problems emerged, while others assumed new guises. This was true the country over. Between 1870 and 1900, college enrollment in the United States increased four times as fast as the population. The national trend was reflected in the rapid growth of Princeton during these years, but Rutgers was not to feel its full effect for another generation, or until its relation to the State was made more explicit.

Not all these students came to college inflamed by the high ideals of a Woodrow Wilson; many, in fact, came for precisely those reasons that Wilson and other foremost scholars deplored: to train for a job, to gain social status, to display athletic prowess, or simply to enjoy four years of pleasant irresponsibility with congenial companions. The Princeton alumnus who complained—apocryphally perhaps—that Wilson was trying to make a grand old college over into a damned institution of learning was typical of many. American universities at the turn of the century were schizophrenic institutions. On the one hand, they proclaimed the highest intellectual ideals and offered ever broader educational opportunities to the few who sought them; on the other, they were weighed down by a largely inert student body, the majority of whom neither cared for nor recognized the pearls that were daily cast before them. Wealth, vulgarly displayed, and the beginnings of a new social stratification based on wealth were having their effects on some campuses; it was the time of Harvard's "gold coast," the time when wealthy young wastrels at Yale considered affairs with Broadway chorus girls as part of the curriculum, and when the administrators at Nassau Hall had to meet charges that Princeton had become a rich man's school where the sons of poor Presbyterian ministers could no longer feel at home. Rutgers, with a smaller and, on the whole, less wealthy constituency, escaped the more severe of these strictures.

Not that students of that era were lazy or lethargic. On the contrary, many were feverishly busy—but not with their studies. Election to the right fraternity or eating club became a paramount consideration. "Activities" were the goal of the ambitious student; whoever wanted to be a big-man-on-the-campus had to work hard at various chores whose connection with the arts and sciences was tenuous: editing the student newspaper, managing the glee club, manipulating campus or fraternity politics, or—greatest glory of all—making the football team. In all this striving, "intellect was no handicap, provided it was tactfully concealed."* But the classroom lost out. That was the place to relax. There, according to Henry Seidel Canby, Yale '99, "we could sit and sit while ideas about evolution or Shakespeare dropped upon us like the gentle rain from heaven, which seeped in or evaporated according to our mental temperatures."**

Overshadowing all other extra-curricular activities, intercollegiate athletics took precedence as the most rewarding activity, and football, which Princeton and Rutgers had inaugurated on that memorable November afternoon in 1869, was the principal sport. It had not yet become big business, complete with million-dollar stadiums, bowl games, and grand-jury investigations, but it was underway. Princeton and Rutgers met again in 1870 and irregularly after that, as the former drifted into the circle of what was to become the Ivy League. Rutgers played Yale in the early 1870's and lost, 3 to 1. At this game, played in New Haven, admission was charged, the losers receiving half of the $160-gate. Rutgers continued to play some Ivy teams, but also found other rivals on the middle-eastern seaboard; it always maintained creditable teams which occasionally, as in the 1920's, rose to national prominence.

The thing that raised athletics to such heights of popularity and gave it status and prestige was of course its competitive character. Higher education, like all American society, was itself competitive, and it was only natural for colleges to try to surpass their peers. One might suppose that the true yardstick for comparative excellence among universities would be intellectual, and at times it was. Both Princeton and Rutgers were members of an association of eastern colleges, in the 1870's, which held contests in classical literatures and in mathematics. A kind of "College Bowl" program

* Samuel E. Morison, *Three Centuries of Harvard* (Cambridge, 1936), 422.

** Henry S. Canby, *Alma Mater* (New York, 1936), 49.

of pre-television days, this association represented a last-gasp attempt to revitalize the old literary and debating societies. The association broke down under competition from other and newer activities. Academic competition, after all, left something to be desired, for it was not conclusive. The evidence for intellectual or, for that matter, ethical or esthetic superiority could not always be interpreted with precision. But when you could pit your best five or nine or eleven men against your rival's best, under conditions agreed upon in advance and subject to the judgment of a disinterested arbiter, superiority was clearly established. You can't argue with the final score. And so competitive sports became an oversimplified symbol of excellence, a college fetish. All the vigor of young manhood, the pride of achievement, the self-effacing loyalties of campus life, and all the nostalgia of alumni were poured into this one channel, and in a flood of sentiment, swept all other values before them. At annual home-coming games old grads stood awkwardly at attention while the strains of "On the Banks" or "Old Nassau" floated through the autumn haze, and even flippant sophomores momentarily felt the pressure of something greater than themselves. The words might be trite, the tune borrowed, but the song bathed the world in a golden glow and stirred new fire in half-forgotten loyalties.

There was no stopping the extra-curricular activities which swept in to fill the vacuum when the inner unity of the old classical college was lost in the multi-purpose university. Neither faculty nor administration tried very hard, for there was something to be said for nearly every one of the new student interests when it first appeared. Only later in their cumulative effect did they become menacing, when the sideshows, as Woodrow Wilson called them, threatened to crowd out the main circus. Rutgers authorities welcomed organized sports, which seemed to offer a suitable way of realizing the old maxim of a sound mind in a sound body. In his history of the college, President Demarest writes of the development of intercollegiate athletics, which came about largely in his administration, with benevolent approval. Here, as elsewhere, the alumni became the chief supporters of athletics. An alumni syndicate headed by a prominent trustee, the railroad tycoon Leonor F. Loree, 1877, gave regular and substantial support to Rutgers sports. The benevolent interest of the trustees even extended to such byproducts as the college colors. A trustees' committee which investigated the matter recommended, for a number of weighty reasons which included even Scriptural warrant, the adoption of scarlet as the Rutgers color.

President McCosh, whose preference was for gymnastics, welcomed football when it first appeared at Princeton, but tried to curb it later to prevent its growing into a Frankenstein's monster. Some said he criticized the overemphasis on competitive sports only when Princeton lost; yet when one student frankly admitted that he had come to college to play football and not to study, McCosh thought the matter sufficiently grave to mention it in his annual report to the trustees. His successor, Francis L. Patton, found it necessary to face down the alarming rumor that he was indifferent to athletics by conspicuously appearing at football practice from time to time. Wilson's intellectualism was condoned and he himself rated high with the students, because it was reported that in his younger days on the Wesleyan faculty he had actually coached the team.

Undeniably, organized athletics provided a new outlet for animal spirits which, in earlier days, had erupted in so many childish pranks and adolescent rowdyism, in both New Jersey college towns. Though fully decorous behavior and Sunday-school manners did not exactly become the rule on either campus, the level of sophistication rose. There were other signs of growing maturity. It was in these years that student self-government began to function. At Rutgers, the first student organization dates back to the early 1890's, and it has persisted through many changes in form to this day. At Princeton, the same student body that worshipped its football heroes also petitioned the faculty to establish the honor system in examinations. The petition was granted; the students assumed responsibility for the integrity of the examinations, and still do. As for Rutgers, the honor system became operative only in the college for women, where student morale was high, the faculty enlightened, and where they did not play football. Honor systems were most successful in women's colleges, which were shiny and new, eager to prove themselves worthy, and not burdened with many years of sinful history.

The two institutions differed in their treatment of fraternities. At Rutgers, where national fraternities had established chapters as early as 1845, the trustees and the faculty gave cautious approval, largely because the residences helped alleviate the acute shortage of dormitory space. Beginning with the Delta Phi House in 1887, fraternity houses multiplied, and though the trustees retained control over their expansion, they became an integral part of campus life. Princeton authorities frowned on fraternities from the time of their first appearance in the 1840's. The secret societies were not fully eradicated however until thirty years later, and then over the bitter protest of the alumni. Meanwhile, innocent little eating clubs had arisen; they were not secret societies, and their membership was limited to juniors and seniors. These met with faculty approval. As they grew, the clubs erected buildings of their own, strung out along Prospect Avenue, to become the Princeton club system, most satisfactory to its members, less so to those who could not get in. When President Wilson, in his effort to reestablish the unity of the university on a higher intellectual level, proposed his quadrangle plan of dormitory living, the clubs felt themselves threatened. Once again the alumni brought pressure; the faculty and trustees showed little enthusiasm for Wilson's plan, and he was defeated. Today, much modified by student and faculty action, and with some of their objectionable features removed, the clubs remain an essential part, and problem, of Princeton campus life.

A final activity worth recording was the proliferation of student publications. Magazines and newspapers had been a perennial outlet for intellectual and esthetic interests left unsatisfied in the classroom. Campus newspapers and periodicals now became "big business;" students aiming at high editorial positions had to take their tasks seriously and give them a good deal of time. The *Nassau Monthly* and the *Daily Princetonian* put in their apearance as well as the *Princeton Alumni Weekly,* the only weekly alumni magazine in America. The *Targum* of Rutgers, founded in 1867, has published without interruption from that day to this. An annual at first, resembling, on a smaller scale, the present-day *Scarlet Letter,* it became a monthly and finally a daily. The *Rutgers Alumni Monthly,* which began as a quarterly, dates from 1914. In short, when literary and debating societies lost favor, talents that might otherwise have been stifled by athletics and fraternity politics found an outlet in writing and publishing.

VI

PRINCETON AND RUTGERS TODAY

NEW JERSEY'S TWO COLONIAL colleges have become thriving American universities, each exemplifying one of the major types of organized higher education in this country. Princeton is an illustrious example of the so-called private university. Independent of direct control by either state or church, it is still governed by the self-perpetuating board of trustees prescribed in the Charter of 1746. Its income is still derived from tuition fees and the return from a very considerable endowment accumulated over the centuries, as well as from regular annual gifts by the alumni and occasional grants for special purposes from government agencies, private industry, and individual friends and well-wishers. Its constituency and reputation are nationwide, though it happens to be located in New Jersey. Rutgers, which started out on the same path, has changed direction to become the State and Land-grant University of New Jersey. Controlled by a state-dominated board of governors, it receives about one-half of its operating expenses from regular annual appropriations by the Legislature. It pieces out the rest with student fees, which at present run considerably lower than in most private universities, and the income from a modest endowment. It also receives annual gifts from loyal alumni, and constantly expanding sums for special purposes from the Federal government, educational foundations, and private industry. Nine-tenths of its students are from

New Jersey and its services are primarily to the State; but in certain areas its contributions extend beyond the state borders and have become national and international in scope.

The State University of New Jersey was 92 years in the making. The process was not completed until 1956, and the final steps, from the Sesquicentennial of 1916, must be explained now. In 1917 the Legislature designated the land-grant part of Rutgers as the State University, and in 1926, two years after changing the name of Rutgers College to Rutgers University, the trustees extended the title to the rest of the institution. The newly-labeled State University included the original Rutgers College, the College of Agriculture (the former scientific school), New Jersey College for Women (now Douglass College), an embryonic graduate school, and professional divisions of engineering, ceramics, and education. There were about eight hundred undergraduates in the colleges for men and half that number in the college for women; there were a handful of graduate students and a summer school with an attendance of about eight hundred, most of them teachers from all parts of New Jersey. Three years after the change of title, the Legislature created a commission to clarify the relations between Rutgers and the State, and the commission in turn directed the attorney-general to submit an opinion for its guidance. In this opinion, which covered the developments since 1864, the attorney-general held that a contractual relation had been established which created mutual responsibilities, and that on this basis "the institution has become literally and virtually, as well as lawfully, the State University of New Jersey." On the strength of this opinion a board of regents was now established to negotiate between the two contracting parties and to supervise the expenditure of the annual appropriation; shortly thereafter, State tuition scholarships, originally introduced in 1864, were greatly increased in number and distributed by counties.

Official relations continued thus, with minor changes,

NASSAU HALL TODAY

Nassau Hall, built in 1756, has successfully survived Revolutionary bombardment, two fires, and the whims of later architects and restorers. It is the best known university building in America.

until 1945, when the Legislature in a formal resolution confirmed all of Rutgers as the State University and the trustees similarly declared that the entire institution was impressed with a public trust. Increased participation by the State in the management of the university was also provided for. Soon after this, in 1948, a state-wide referendum was held on a fifty-million-dollar bond issue for capital expenditures, the money to be distributed among the State University, the six State teachers' colleges, and the Department of Institutions and Agencies. To the dismay of Rutgers and its friends, the vote went against the bond issue by a majority of about five to four. True, the issues were complex, yet even when allowance was made for extraneous factors and for that fairly constant percentage of citizens who consistently vote against all bond issues, the rebuff at the polls seemed to indicate that the people in New Jersey had not yet wholeheartedly accepted Rutgers as their state university, in the way in which the citizens of Wisconsin or California accepted theirs.

In retrospect, a variety of reasons suggest themselves for the setback. In the first place, the New Jersey of 1948 was not the New Jersey of 1864, when the association with the State began. Then it was fairly homogeneous state, of English, Scottish, and Dutch stock, predominantly agricultural, and overwhelmingly Protestant. By 1948 it had become an industrial state and the population had increased tenfold. Moreover, this larger population was heterogeneous and diversified, for heavy immigration from many European countries had fundamentally changed the racial and national proportions of the earlier date. Religious pluralism had accompanied racial diversity and New Jersey had become, like all of eastern and urban America, a body of citizens differing widely in national origins and religious affiliations. This modern New Jersey was apparently not ready to accept as its state university an institution of colonial antecedents, historically identified with a national and religious element which had now shrunk to a minority.

Though the university had long since freed itself of all legal ties to any church or ethnic group, the historical image persisted.

Meantime, other colleges and universities had been founded in New Jersey under Methodist, Roman Catholic, Lutheran, and non-sectarian private auspices. They all had their loyal supporters, some of whom considered the near-monopoly of public funds which Rutgers enjoyed as something less than distributive justice. In addition to such vested interests there were thoughtful, public-spirited citizens, not at all unfriendly to Rutgers, for whom the chief stumbling-block was the private, self-perpetuating board of trustees. Public representation on this board, they believed, was not enough; in a true state university there must be public control.

The Rutgers family—students, faculty, administration, and alumni—was not of one mind on this issue. Among the alumni especially there was opposition to State affiliation. Some of the dissenters believed their Alma Mater would have done better to exploit its colonial heritage and remain an independent university, and there were lingering regrets over its failure to become identified with the nebulous but prestige-conferring Ivy League. Nor did the administration always pursue a consistent policy. President Demarest remained lukewarm toward State affiliation, but his successor, John M. Thomas, came in as an enthusiastic proponent of the idea. In his inaugural address President Thomas made his far-reaching plans unmistakably clear and during the first year of his administration, 1925-1926, he gave some sixty public addresses emphasizing the services of Rutgers to New Jersey and characterizing it as a "State University in process of development." Thomas was president for only five years; a cooling of his possibly premature enthusiasm was noticeable under his successor, Robert C. Clothier. Holding office throughout the critical depression and war decades, President Clothier took his stand, with full approbation of the trustees, on the attorney-general's opinion of 1927. In other words he held that

Rutgers and the State were two independent entities, each capable of managing without the other but bound by a contractual agreement to provide adequately for the needs of higher education, an agreement which both parties must honor. He pictured Rutgers and the State as partners, and while holding the University scrupulously to its commitments under the partnership, he insisted on its integrity as guaranteed by its charter. A graduate of Princeton, Clothier was aware of the advantages of an independent university.

The abstract question of legal status was complicated in the early 1930's by a shortage of funds. The annual appropriations, which had been running close to a million dollars, were reduced again and again by a harassed Legislature, itself under pressure from unemployed and depression-ridden citizens. After a third such reduction, which seriously crippled essential university functions, President Clothier protested courteously but firmly against this last unkindest cut of all by pointing out that Rutgers had thrown its full seventeen millions of assets into the service of the State and was entitled to better treatment in return. He hoped, he said, for a "friendly and understanding" relationship in the future. His hopes were not completely dashed, nor yet entirely realized. The uneasy partnership continued; appropriations increased again as business improved, and reached considerably higher levels after the war. Yet, on the other hand, opposition to the partnership remained alive, and was apparent in the defeat of the bond issue mentioned above.

At long last the trustees took the bull by the horns and faced the fundamental issue: the ambivalent status of Rutgers as an independent, privately controlled corporation which at the same time claimed to be the State University. By this time President Clothier had retired; his successor, Lewis Webster Jones, who came to Rutgers from a western state university, pressed for full public status, taking up where Thomas had left off. A trustees' committee was now appointed, headed by the late Lansing P. Shield, an enthusiastic proponent of a state university. After carefully investigating the legal, historical, and other pertinent aspects of the issue, this committee drew up an amendment to the charter which would shift control to the State. The amendment created a board of governors to be composed of six members appointed by the governor with the consent of the senate, five members chosen by and from the existing board of trustees, plus the president of the university and the state commissioner of education *ex officiis*. The trustees adopted this self-denying proposal, the Legislature approved, and Rutgers became a public corporation, directed by the new board of governors, while the original board of trustees continued as legal owners of the property and served otherwise in an advisory capacity. Thus ended the long process begun in 1864, and Rutgers became the State University in a manner unique in the history of American higher education. The year was 1956.

Clothed in its new garment of civic righteousness, Rutgers once again appealed for sorely needed capital funds. With the cooperation of the commissioner of education, now a member of the new board of governors, the appeal was enlarged to include the six state colleges—the former teachers' colleges—as well as the Newark College of Engineering, which had been receiving state aid for years. Once again the Legislature authorized a referendum, this time on a bond issue of sixty million dollars for capital expenditure for public higher education, of which Rutgers was to get twenty-nine millions. And this time the vote was favorable. Chief among the factors contributing to this reversal at the polls was no doubt the new legal status of Rutgers, now shown to be, in a systematic campaign of enlightenment by its supporters, unimpeachably the State University. Then too, all the forces of public higher education made common cause for the first time. Most valuable, finally, was the support of the leading private university in the state. When President Goheen of Princeton issued a public statement in favor of the bond issue as the best means of dealing with the problems of higher education in New Jersey, the prestige of Princeton was thrown into its support, and this proved a tremendous asset.

Like New Jersey itself, Rutgers and Princeton are in many ways new institutions today, for all their history and tradition. In physical appearance, to begin with, both have undergone marked changes, especially in recent years. Rutgers, with new construction fairly exploding on all its campuses, would hardly be recognized by a graduate of twenty, or even ten, years ago. Old Queen's still stands, but to its original downtown campus of fifty acres there have been added, piecemeal since 1864, some nine hundred acres on the south side of New Brunswick where the sprawling campus of Douglass College is located and behind it the College of Agriculture with its experimental farm extending far into the county. Still newer is the eight-hundred-acre University Heights campus on the left bank of the Raritan, which contains the football stadium, other athletic fields, and the new science center. Then there are the undergraduate college and the professional schools of Newark Rutgers, planning a building program coordinated with the urban renewal project there. The last addition to the far-flung University campus is the College of South Jersey, where plans for expansion are similarly geared to Camden's rebuilding program. In thus acquiring branches in the most populous regions of the State, Rutgers is following the current practice of state universities, all of which feel an obligation to make their services available, with the least inconvenience, to the greatest number of citizens.

Princeton is under no such obligation. Its campus therefore, though ample for its needs, remains where it has always been, radiating east, south, and west from Nassau Hall. The Hall, while still useful and historically significant, must share the spotlight today with scores of structures of all shapes, sizes, and architectural designs, which have been added since the early nineteenth

THE RUTGERS UNIVERSITY LIBRARY

Opened in 1956, this library houses over 600,000 volumes, while other special libraries bring the total number to over one million. As at Princeton, students have access to the stacks.

century. In this casual accumulation of buildings Princeton, like Rutgers, is typical. No better laboratories exist for the study of American architecture than university campuses, especially those that extend back to colonial times. There the fortunes of each institution, the fat and the lean years, are as distinctly recorded by the style of architecture that predominates as the life-span of the giant sequoia in its annual rings. They are all on view, from the colonial Georgian of the oldest building, through the classical revival, on to the red-brown arches and slit windows of Henry Hobson Richardson, and to other Victorian adaptations. In the twentieth century the universities turned to neo-Gothic or a second round of pink and white Georgian, and finally to the severe functional glass and concrete modes of recent years. In addition to these recognizable styles, most campuses exhibit some of those formless monstrosities that have been variously described as railroad-depot or firehouse style, French-and-Indian renaissance, and Custer's Last Stand. Unlike business and industry, where profits are the chief goal, colleges cannot readily tear down the old just because the new is more efficient. Sentiment plays a part too, and alumni may be heard from if ruthless hands are laid on sacred halls. As for functionalism, virtually every new style was recommended in its day as both functionally and esthetically superior to its immediate predecessor. In all probability the next generation will shake its head over the stark austerity and the lack of beauty of mid-twentieth-century structures and will regard our glass-and-aluminum slabs on stilts with the same sophisticated condescension that we now bestow on the Tudor and Georgian frills of the generation before ours.

Princeton had happily started out with perhaps the finest, certainly the largest, college building in British North America. The earliest additions, Stanhope Hall, Philosophical Hall, and East and West College, were carried out in the same sober design as Nassau Hall. Then the college was briefly touched by the Greek revival, when the twin Ionic temples of Clio and Whig were erected. Thereafter, in McCosh's day, the college went in heavily for neo-Romanesque with its ponderous arches, round towers, and general over-ornateness. At the turn of the century, the university committed itself to the Tudor Gothic style as revived by Ralph Adams Cram and his school, and that became the dominant note of its campus. The great dormitory quadrangles, the soaring chapel, the graduate school—all this, in the first half of the twentieth century, *was* Princeton, and gave it, in the words of Woodrow Wilson, an additional thousand years of history. But this era too is coming to an end. The magnificent Harvey S. Firestone library still bears a family resemblance to the Tudor ensemble, but this is not true of such recent structures as the Forrestal Laboratory, Wilcox Hall, the Engineering Quadrangle, and the projected new buildings of the graduate school. Traditionalists, on and off the campus, have protested, but if history is any guide their protests will not hold back the tide of change.

At Rutgers, physical expansion was slower. By the end of the nineteenth century Old Queen's, serene and dignified, found itself surrounded by a motley array of structures, mongrels all of them, and apparently built for the ages. All are still in use. In the twentieth century, soon after Princeton had gone in for Gothic, Rutgers adopted the Georgian, an authentic American college style with colonial antecedents. This style is seen at its most characteristic in the gymnasium of 1930, the dormitories of that period, and most of the buildings of Douglass College and the College of Agriculture. But Georgian too is now giving way to "modern." The great new University Library and the post-World-War-II high-rise dormitories along the Raritan still retain a sense of the Georgian: red brick with white stone facings; but characteristic decorations and other marks of recognition have been sloughed off, in a kind of architectural strip-tease, until only the functional essentials remain. And in the new complex of science buildings on University Heights the Georgian is being entirely discarded. True, the microbiology building still clings to the style, thanks largely to the zeal of a trustee who held anything short of pure Georgian subversive, but such recent structures as the Nuclear Science Center have gone completely modern. Inevitably so, for the work that goes on in them is as novel and unprecedented as the buildings that house it.

Turning from the physical structure to the inner life of the two universities, we find considerable similarity in their organization and activities, as one would expect, but also distinctive differences. In both, the original college of arts and sciences continues to function, along with a graduate school and a wide assortment of professional schools. But the emphasis differs. Princeton, not beholden to the citizens of New Jersey with all their various needs and demands, has had greater freedom of choice in deciding what kind of an institution it wishes to be. It has chosen to offer a liberal and scientific education of high quality to a very select student body. It offers this education to the qualified few under the most advantageous circumstances. The facilities and equipment in dormitories, laboratories, and libraries are excellent and verge on the luxurious. A Princeton education is expensive and a large proportion of the student body comes from well-to-do homes. Yet there are liberal scholarships. In recent years more than one-third of the undergraduates and as high as ninety percent of the graduate students have been receiving financial aid.

The gap between rich and poor is an old story at Princeton; the situation has frequently been a matter for concern, and remedies were sought by presidents from McCosh all the way back to Samuel Stanhope Smith. But then, quality is always expensive, and that is what the University stresses, rather than quantity; mass production and assembly-line techniques have no place on the Princeton campus. Small discussion groups—the precepts which Woodrow Wilson introduced—bring students and faculty members together for informal examination of issues and ideas. The preceptorial system is an integral part of a Princeton education. The four-course program, with independent study culminating in a senior thesis, has the same end in view.

A faculty bristling with scholars of national repute is at the disposal of the undergraduates; the same faculty guides graduate students to the doctorate in most fields of the humanities and the sciences. Professional schools and divisions are not as numerous as in a large state university, for here again the private university has greater freedom to select and reject. Princeton has concentrated on such areas as engineering, art and archaeology, architecture, international affairs, and nuclear physics. The Woodrow Wilson School of Public and International Affairs and the Forrestal Research Center are household words in academic and scientific circles. Yet for all its achievements in the growing graduate and professional programs, Princeton continues to focus on the undergraduate: he still comes first. Unlike some of the other Ivy League universities, where the original college, overshadowed by a multitude of professional and graduate schools and institutes, has been reduced to a minor part of the whole, Princeton still considers its three thousand college students its major concern. There is perhaps no other university in the country where such a distinguished faculty gives so much of its time to the undergraduates. The desired end-product is still a liberal education, as it was from the days of Witherspoon. Presidents of the last half-century have all adhered to it. "The chief end of education is the making of a man," whose main vocation is to play his part in the community of his fellows. It is "the personal quest for knowledge and rational self-mastery." The faculty contributes to this end by "effective teaching and productive scholarship." *

The full stature of the University and its impact on the

* The three quoted passages are, in that order, from the Inaugural Addresses of Presidents John Grier Hibben (1912), Robert F. Goheen (1958), and Harold W. Dodds (1933).

world of higher education were revealed in the Bicentennial Celebration, which ran through the entire academic year of 1946-1947. The opening service, conducted by the Archbishop of Canterbury, gave proof that the little provincial Presbyterian college of the eighteenth century had come a long way. The impressive list of lectures, symposia, conferences, and convocations of that year was further proof. While occasions of this kind offer some insight, it is impossible to do justice to the many kinds of research and scholarly activity that go on simultaneously on a campus such as Princeton's. One typical project is a definitive edition of the writings of Thomas Jefferson, which was begun two years before the Bicentennial and is still going on. Quite different in nature, yet of tremendous importance for the Nation's future is the atomic research going on in the Forrestal Center. Over the years, other educational and cultural institutions have found their way to Princeton. First among these was the Theological Seminary of the Presbyterian Church. More recently, the Westminster Choir College has come to town, as has the famous Institute for Advanced Study, where world-renowned figures can settle down for a season to write, to experiment, or just to think. Even private industries in town, like those devising educational tests or conducting public opinion polls, have an academic flavor.

Rutgers, in its capacity as State University, has been moving in another direction. Not that there are any fundamental differences between it and its New Jersey neighbor. Its main purpose, like that of Princeton or, for that matter, of any university worthy of the name, is the discovery and transmission of organized knowledge: research and teaching. Its human products are men and women with disciplined minds and specialized skills. In translating these abstract aims into concrete programs of action, however, and in deciding what to do first, what to emphasize, what to postpone or ignore, Rutgers is guided by other considerations: the priorities are not the same. The State University must above all else satisfy the needs of the people of New Jersey. This overriding fact explains the complex organization of the university, the heterogeneous character of its many subdivisions, and the emphasis upon extension services as well as resident instruction. The subdivisions produce a formidable list. Those in New Brunswick include, in addition to the original men's college and the college for women, numerous schools, institutes, and divisions which provide training in such widely diversified fields as agriculture, ceramics, engineering, journalism, library science, nursing, practical politics, social work, and teacher education. A school of medicine is in view, thanks to an initial one-million-dollar grant from the W. K. Kellogg Foundation. The graduate school, though still without a building, centers in New Brunswick, close to the main university library. An alert university press rounds out the New Brunswick educational compound.

Newark Rutgers, conveniently located in the State's largest city, has its own College of Arts and Sciences, as well as the university's Law School and School of Business Administration. All three were originally separate and private; they combined in the 1930's as the University of Newark, and were merged with Rutgers in 1946. The College of South Jersey in Camden, similarly acquired in 1950, brings the services of the University to the southern counties of the State. Finally, and increasingly important, there is the rapidly growing field of adult education, in two divisions, with courses conducted in all parts of the State. University College offers a wide range of subjects which, if studied in proper sequence and combination, will lead to a regular Rutgers degree; while University Extension courses are designed for those who wish merely to enlarge their knowledge and understanding of the world about them, or to acquire some skill or competence, and do not desire a degree or academic credit. All told, over twenty-two thousand students were enrolled in degree programs in the

State University in 1962-1963; about one-half of these were undergraduates in New Brunswick, Newark, and Camden.

This University, with all its ramifications and all its resources, is the keystone of New Jersey's system of higher education. It has been so designated in the recent Strayer Report, an analysis of services and estimate of future needs made by a group of experts under the leadership of the late Dr. George D. Strayer at the direction of the State Board of education. In all its schools and colleges, about a thousand professors and research specialists are at work, teaching, lecturing, experimenting, publishing: a tremendous expansion, in numbers and functions, of the classical-philosophical faculty of eight or nine in the Rutgers of a hundred years ago, whose main and almost exclusive business was teaching languages, mathematics, and philosophy to a hundred boys.

The ways in which a state university can serve society are numerous, the by-products and fringe benefits almost infinite. A few samples must suffice to illustrate this wider and indefinite area:

Every year Rutgers receives a large number of foreign students who come, usually, to acquire some highly specialized knowledge or skill to take back to their homelands.

Rutgers conducts a graduate school of banking, for years the only one in the country, to which bank officials and employes come from all states in the Union for an intensive period of study every June.

Research in microbiology in the College of Agriculture resulted in the discovery of streptomycin with its incalculable benefits.

In 1947, the University was host to the State Constitutional Convention. Throughout that hot summer, the delegates labored on the campus, holding their main sessions in the gymnasium. As permanent chairman they elected the President of the University, Robert C. Clothier. With skill and devotion he ironed out differences and carried the assembly through many a precarious situation in a way that none of the political leaders present could have done. His "devoted leadership, sound judgment, and personal integrity," in the words of the Resolution of Appreciation passed on the last day, contributed mightily to the successful outcome of this historic event.

And now New Jersey's two universities, which have shared its history as Colony and as State, are about to enter the last third of the twentieth century, carrying with them the hopes of thousands, in and out of the State. If the record of two hundred years means anything, these hopes will not be disappointed. Both have rich assets, not only of physical property, but in human resources. Both have sound leadership, for they have consistently chosen academicians as presidents ever since the professional theologian went out of fashion. Neither has succumbed to the lure of glamorous personalities, chosen from business, politics, or military life to become titular heads and thus confer a specious prestige and shed an uncertain luster on staid and sober academic enterprises. On the contrary, both have consistently chosen their chief executives from the ranks of scholars and administrators. Seasoned deans, or professors of Greek or philosophy or economics or political science with demonstrated qualities of leadership have risen to the top and successfully combined the academic with the practical. Princeton's President today, Robert F. Goheen, is a classical scholar who can dazzle his trustees with annual reports oriented upon Heraclitus and Parmenides, yet who is in such close touch with current educational issues that he is chosen president of the American Council on Education, an eminently practical body. The President of Rutgers is a former professor of philosophy who holds degrees from Cambridge and Harvard universities and came from the faculty of Columbia University. Mason W. Gross can write learnedly about Alfred Whitehead's philosophy of adventure and also keep his finger on the public pulse; he speaks with authority on all manner of academic and civic occasions and knows what a twentieth-century state university is for.

To keep their universities abreast of the times both presidents must, as college presidents have always done, look to the finances. Here their problems are not the same. Princeton, though one of the most favored of the hundreds of private colleges and universities, still must support itself entirely from tuition fees, income from endowment, sponsored research grants, and gifts from friends and foundations. There is widespread concern today for the future of these independent colleges which must scrounge and scramble for support in an intensely competitive market, and at a time when rising costs reduce the value of gifts while mounting taxes tend to reduce their size. But however doubtful the future may look for private colleges generally, Princeton at the moment is in no danger of financial collapse. In 1958 a campaign was launched for fifty-three million dollars to augment the University's capital resources. When it ended, four years later, sixty million dollars had been subscribed, and an additional thirty-five million had been given by anonymous donors to the Woodrow Wilson School. What is more remarkable: though much of this new endowment came from alumni, the regular annual gifts did not fall off during those four years but continued unabated. These recurring annual gifts, now amounting to well over a million dollars a year, have more than once made the difference between a deficit and a surplus.

Rutgers' sources of income are somewhat different. As the State University it can count on a regular annual appropriation of public funds, which at present covers about one-half of the cost of running the university. This adds an element of stability to its finances, but tuition fees, endowment income, and gifts and grants are still needed to make up the rest. Besides, the Legislature does not appropriate as much as the administration requests: no state legislature ever does. New Jersey, a State with one of the highest per capita incomes in the Nation, is not among the leaders in its per capita support of higher education. Yet Rutgers has thus far been spared the irresponsible, punitive, and politically inspired cuts with which legislatures in other states occasionally hamstring their institutions of higher learning.

But money is only a means to an end: it makes the work of higher education possible. There are those who contend that a privately controlled university, once its finances are in order, has greater freedom of action than a public institution. The particular kind of freedom meant here is known in the language of the profession as academic freedom. This means the right of scholars, teachers, and specialists to pursue their research and work out their theories unhampered by government, church, or pressure groups of any kind, and to proclaim these theories and to publish the results of their investigations freely, without censorship or suppression. Academic freedom is a university's most precious possession. It is constantly subject to attack from pressure groups, vested interests, and even benefactors and supporters; it can be subtly diminished when the university, subordinating its own concerns to the general welfare in times of crisis, emphasizes one form of activity or one point of view, and reduces or eliminates another. On the whole, both Princeton and Rutgers have maintained their resilience and integrity in the face of pressures of various kinds. During World War II, to cite but one recent example, both put aside their normal activities, reorganized their program, and revolutionized their campus life at the suggestion of the Federal Government, in the overriding interest of national defense. Yet when the war ended and Federal pressures relaxed, both returned to their peacetime educational tasks, their purposes intact and their freedom unimpaired.

There is some logical and historical warrant for the assumption that private universities, having fewer masters, fare better than the state institutions in preserving and exercising academic freedom. The state university operates in the spotlight of glaring publicity. Every taxpayer considers it his university and rightly so. Every pressure group, whether of organized labor, organized business, or organized religion, wants a hearing in the groves of academe for its interests and its philosophy; parents are sensitive to the ideas their sons and daughters encounter in the classroom; and every sports enthusiast knows exactly what is wrong with the football team. But that is democracy. A public university is founded on the supposition that the public has a legitimate interest in its affairs; this alone gives it the right to spend public funds. Democracy can be abused. State universities have at times been subjected to exasperating pressures, which have made it extremely difficult for them to function as centers of the search for truth. Yet on the other hand, some of our better state universities have fought through to positions of considerable freedom and today rank with the best of the independent institutions. The quality of a state university depends in the long run on the quality of the citizens of the state. The citizenry need not be homogeneous—New Jersey's certainly is not. But if the voters are literate, reasonably free from provincialism, and in touch with national and international affairs, and if the university adheres to its business of investigating, informing, and enlightening, it will in most cases be allowed to exercise the freedom which alone justifies its existence.

Even under the most favorable conditions, however, a state university is subject to more harassment than an institution of wealth and renown directed by a self-perpetuating board of trustees in which its own graduates predominate, and it may well be that Princeton in the years ahead will have smoother sailing in matters of academic freedom than Rutgers. Yet Rutgers excels in another kind of freedom: it has greater flexibility to experiment and innovate. Its growing student body, fed by constantly larger high school classes, is a powerful incentive for more courses and for new programs whose extent and proliferation are limited only by the Legislature's willingness to support them. Princeton, on the other hand, with a controlled student enrollment and an income not geared to population figures, must carefully weigh and select every additional course and new program within the framework of its existing resources and limitations. And so, between these two New Jersey institutions, advantages and disadvantages tend to balance out.

Problems remain, and will continue to plague the authorities. One of the most urgent, especially for Rutgers, is that of stretching the resources of the institution to meet the growing number of applicants for admission. According to the Strayer study, the State University will have to increase its enrollment two-and-a-half times by 1970 if it is to meet the legitimate educational needs of the young people of the state. This is a staggering figure. The new buildings, classrooms, laboratories, and library facilities which such increases will necessitate are difficult to visualize. One thing is certain: they will make tremendous demands on the State budget. The cost will increase more than proportionally, for new educational techniques and equipment, in all of which the state university must keep abreast, will raise the unit cost. Among such new techniques is educational television, which requires costly installations, whatever its ultimate advantages. Electronic computers are rapidly becoming indispensable in subject after subject, and they are not to be had at bargain rates. And the latest equipment for teaching and research in nuclear physics runs into astronomic costs. Unless the University can count on the necessary appropriations from the State to meet this steadily increasing demand for its services, it will have to face the alternative of cutting admissions drastically and turning away thousands of New Jersey high school graduates, who will then have to go without a college education or try to find it elsewhere.

Another problem—one connected with the sensitive issue of academic freedom—has suddenly grown formidable. The rapidly mounting volume of subsidies from the Federal government for sponsored research has raised the specter of Federal control. These subsidies may be grants to the university directly for specified purposes or to individual faculty members for approved projects. At Rutgers in 1961-1962, grants and contracts from the Federal government exceeded four million dollars, about one-tenth of the total budget. At Princeton the proportion has gone much higher. The *Princeton Alumni Weekly* recently startled its readers with figures indicating that over half the University's income for 1962-1963, or about twenty-one million dollars, came from Federal sources. Though President Goheen corrected the figure to forty-seven percent and pointed out that two-thirds of this went to the Forrestal Center, the figures were still alarming enough to cause widespread concern among alumni over the possible loss in independence and growing subservience to the Federal government. A lengthy report by the President in the April 19, 1963 issue of the *Alumni Weekly* made the following points: Federal subsidies offer great benefits, but also present serious pitfalls. As long as there is sufficient institutional self-discipline; as long as the money represents payment for specific undertakings underwritten by scholars, is lavished on the physical sciences rather than on the more controversial humanities and social sciences, and is not allowed to interfere with general educational aims, Federal aid can be highly beneficial. For it expands the frontiers of knowledge and advances the National interest, and it promotes the kind of scientific inquiries that can be pursued more fruitfully by a university than by private industry or a government agency.

Both universities would probably admit that the benefits of Federal grants are great. Nevertheless the pressures are there and will increase as subsidies increase; and only rigorous self-discipline and constant watchfulness will ward off the creeping controls.

Foremost among the things that make a university great is a faculty of distinguished scholars. To secure and hold a sufficient number of the ablest professional men and women is a major problem of every university. But there are many universities in the United States, and prestige-conferring "name" scholars are few. Since there are not enough nationally-known productive scholars in the humanities and research specialists in the sciences to go around, the competition is intense. Yet the two New Jersey institutions must get their share of such people to be and remain first-class universities. This is doubly true since both are building up their graduate schools where productive research scholars make their major impact. Princeton now has almost a thousand students in its graduate school, as against three thousand undergraduates. The latest report from Rutgers shows doctoral programs in 41 areas, and over forty-eight hundred graduate students enrolled in the various schools, as opposed to ten thousand full-time undergraduates. By all legitimate means, both universities must attract the best available scholars to their ranks and hold them.

Once such an elite faculty has been acquired, the question arises of its most efficient use. Shall these high-powered people teach undergraduates or graduates, or both? Should they do much teaching at all? There is a growing tendency in leading universities to reduce the teaching-load of their most distinguished professors to a point where only a small number of students, and those mostly graduates plus a few seniors, have any contact with them at all. One course is often all that is required of them, and this is repeatedly interrupted by visits to other universities for special lectures, by professional meetings, or by consultations in Washington with Federal officials. What the university expects from such men is the prestige of their names and the products of their research. The undergraduates meanwhile are left to the ministrations of cheap labor, as the many sections of required courses are turned over to young instructors or graduate students. Both New Jersey universities have a tradition of effective teaching and of concern for the undergraduate, and this should stand them in good stead if they ever need to take a stand against the costly window-dressing of big names.

If a university cannot be great without a first-rate faculty, it is no university at all without students. Student life at Rutgers and Princeton today varies with the character of the institution. Princeton remains what it has always been: a residential college for men, with virtually all its students housed in campus dormitories. Rutgers, which never had a dormitory before 1890, has gone in for campus living in recent years with a vast dormitory building program, and today ninety percent of the women and sixty percent of the men on the New Brunswick campuses are housed in college buildings. But there are no dormitories in Newark or Camden, and all students in those sectors of the State University must commute to their classes. This in itself makes for looser ties and is bound to produce a student body differently oriented from one that lives on the premises twenty-four hours a day. There are other differences. The Princeton undergraduate body is more homogeneous. It was formerly recruited largely from families in the upper economic brackets, and admission still confers social prestige; Princeton, like Yale and Harvard, can skim the cream of the private preparatory schools and the better public high schools. With far more applicants than it can accommodate, this university is in a position to select the ablest and thus to keep its academic standards high. In short, the eight hundred freshmen who enter Princeton every September are a highly intelligent and privileged group of young men.

The best students at Rutgers, the Henry Rutgers scholars, for example, and the high honors candidates at Douglass, are as good as they come, but the student body in general represents a wider range of admissions from high school classes. In recent years about one-half of the applicants to the freshman class have been admitted. At Douglass, where space and facilities are more limited, the selectivity is greater. Those who do gain admission "come from farms, from city homes, from suburbia, from homes of relative wealth and from those where the payment of college tuition is a heavy drain on family finances. . . . They are the sons and daughters of doctors and farmers, miners and carpenters, policemen, school teachers and bricklayers. They represent every level of American life." * A sprinkling of colonial Dutch names which made up the old Rutgers is still found in the rosters of students and faculty, but these names are lost among the multitudes. In one thing Rutgers is fortunate. It is not required, as many state universities are, to admit every state high school graduate, regardless of class standing or college aptitude—a wasteful procedure, both educationally and financially.

Nothing conveys the flavor of campus life better than student newspapers, in this case The *Daily Princetonian* and The *Daily Targum*. The former is an independent financial venture and sells at ten cents a copy; the latter is subsidized by a student activities fee and distributed free. Both get additional revenue from advertising, though the notices in *Targum,* one of the oldest American college newspapers, are not as picturesque as in the early days, when they ranged all the way from Tiffany's on Fifth Avenue to Temperance Billiard Parlors in New Brunswick.

Campus issues predominate, naturally, in the news and editorial columns, but the outside world is not neglected. Both papers carry news reports, feature stories, and occasional editorials dealing with national and international affairs, especially those of a controversial nature and those impinging on college interests. During the State gubernatorial campaign of 1961 the *Princetonian* supported the Republican candidate, while *Targum* leaned to the Democratic side. Each probably reflected majority sentiment among its readers. Both papers transmit a lively awareness of the issues of the day and reflect the willingness of many students to take a stand. The intimidation of the McCarthy era is only a bad dream to the present college generation; the Korean War

* Who Goes to Rutgers?" *Report from Rutgers* (October, 1962).

and World War II, ancient history. The burning causes espoused by today's campus liberals are racial equality and nuclear disarmament. At the same time, both campuses have seen the resurgence of organized conservatives who are making their influence felt, in marked contrast to the political climate of a quarter century ago. Then, the liberal left tended to be radical, while today's trend is toward the radicalism of the extreme right. Between these two opposites, now as then, the uncommitted majority jogs along, busy with its own affairs, and berated by student leaders for its apathy.

Apathy or not, student elections came in for a great deal of attention, even though the editor of the *Princetonian* seemed to disapprove of the rough and tumble of campus politics. "A scholarly gentleman," he announced, "does not campaign at all." It does not appear that he found much support in the Undergraduate Council. In the Rutgers Student Council elections, *Targum* campaigned openly, but not quite persuasively enough, for the candidate of its choice. Much space was given to perennial campus problems. Club membership, with its long history of tension between special privilege and equal opportunity, received its annual share of attention in the *Princetonian,* while at Rutgers the fraternities found themselves under fire, as often before, from the administration and the non-Greek majority. Both papers aired controversial issues, served as forums for unpopular causes and as vehicles of protest against unpopular actions of the administration. When resentment against the latter reached the boiling point it was usually directed against the deans, who always make convenient scapegoats. Presidents and faculties, by and large, remained popular.

Student pranks and horseplay, while less prominent than in the bucolic years, still make the headlines now and then. However, intercollegiate athletics still appear, from the amount of space devoted to sports, to be the most exciting extra-curricular activity. This is perhaps more true of Princeton than of Rutgers, where multiple campuses and the higher percentage of day students tend to dampen the fervor. It was a matter of great concern to the *Princetonian,* for example, that tickets for games in Palmer Stadium were to be reallocated for the benefit of the alumni, presumably at the expense of the students; again, the paper made much of a systematic "hate Yale" campaign, complete with rallies and banners. This last seemed a bit forced and synthetic, and it is just possible that the former football hero who wrote an indignant letter complaining of the decline of the sport since his day had a point. Yet Rutgers, too, experienced a thrill that shook the oldest alumnus and the newest freshman when the football team in 1961 had the first undefeated season in its entire history—a history which goes back, like that of Princeton, to 1869. For the latter it has been a distinguished history, for there were great days when the team, in seasons in which it defeated both Harvard and Yale, could claim a mythical national championship. Those days are gone. As a member of the Ivy League, which has come to recognize the evils inherent in commercialized college athletics, Princeton adheres to a code of partial de-emphasis, has curbed the more reprehensible practices, and has set up standards of scholastic integrity for its athletes, so that there is no necessary conflict today between academic excellence and athletic prowess.

Rutgers University, though not a member, maintains Ivy League standards in its control of athletics. Its varsity teams must be academically respectable; some of its best players have been Henry Rutgers scholars. Yet it faces a problem. As a state university growing in size and importance, it will be subjected to pressure from the perennial adolescents among its alumni and from well-wishers throughout New Jersey to go in for "major league" football, like most state universities. The Rutgers administration knows, of course, as anyone can know who views national collegiate athletics in perspective, that a top-flight football team does not make a great university. Harvard's football prowess is not what it once was, yet Harvard's intellectual luster remains undimmed. The University of California at Berkeley, with nine Nobel prize-winners on its faculty, will survive the latter-day decline of its football fortunes. The University of Notre Dame has been less frequently found among the top ten football teams in recent years, but its stature as an academic institution has been growing steadily.

In that major scandal of American higher education which is commercialized athletics, Princeton and Rutgers, who unwittingly started it all, are far from being the worst offenders. Both maintain honest academic standards, and neither makes open financial proposals to every beefy bone-crusher and gangling giant in high school senior classes who offers his talents for sale to the highest collegiate bidder. At the same time, neither university has made any move to roll back the sport to what it was when they first met on the football field in 1869: not a profit-making public spectacle, but a *game,* of, by, and for the students, subsidized only to the extent that it promotes the health and welfare of all. There are some great American universities which have done just that.

In the two student newspapers, then, the whole kaleidoscope of undergraduate life, gay and serious, trivial and profound, passes in review. In one, the daily grist may range from football concerns to a discussion of the ideal size of precepts or reports on lectures by world-famous scholars, or to the sensation produced by the first woman enrolled in the graduate school. The other may give much space to a student vote for girl cheerleaders, but will also discuss the functions of the university press or insist editorially on the right to bring in speakers for unpopular causes. Most gratifying are the many instances, in the files of both, of their awareness of the real purposes of a university. Thus one issue of the *Princetonian* carried a special supplement devoted to the arts at the university; on another occasion it published, with approval, an open letter from the president on the importance of resisting all pressures for conformity and of safeguarding the right of every student to be different and even unpopular. The same note is sounded in *Targum*. There is, for example, the half-facetious letter arguing against the proposal to "militarize" the band after the fashion of the huge quick-stepping bands of other institutions which perform their acrobatics between halves. The writer is pleased with the present Rutgers band, which has no oppressive discipline, is casual, and does not always march in a straight line, but enjoys itself. This, he thinks, is in keeping with University and National ideals, and he hopes that neither will ever be regimented. In a similar vein a *Targum* editorial commends Rutgers as a haven for the individual, requiring no conformity in dress, behavior, or ideas.*

If this assessment of campus life is reasonably accurate, it seems fair to assert that the students of New Jersey's two oldest universities are moving, with much zig-zagging and some backsliding, toward the same goal at which faculties and administrations have been aiming for two hundred years: a liberal education. Today in twentieth-century terms, this means the orderly investigation of facts and ideas in all fields, the critical evaluation of our culture, and the right of the individual within this disciplined framework to be himself. To achieve these ends is a university's principal business. Aware of their heritage and clear in their aims, Princeton and Rutgers, though steeped in tradition and heavy with history, can look confidently to the next hundred years.

* This sampling of the two papers is from the academic year 1961-1962.

BIBLIOGRAPHICAL NOTE

Colleges and universities usually keep voluminous records, and Princeton and Rutgers are no exceptions. Both have extensive archives which occupy considerable space in their libraries. Though not complete for the early years, when Rutgers moved about a lot and Princeton had fires, the records of both are remarkably full and abundant for a study of this kind.

The core of official college documents consists of trustees' minutes, faculty minutes, presidents' reports, and annual catalogues. On the student side we have the various undergraduate publications: periodicals of varying types and lengths, year books, and, in recent years, daily newspapers. In addition there are the alumni publications. The libraries have their outlets too: the *Princeton University Library Chronicle* and the *Journal of the Rutgers University Library*. The Princeton University Press and the Rutgers University Press are not primarily concerned with the history of their institutions, but with the promotion and publication of scholarly research in all fields.

There are histories of both universities and I have made extensive use of them, especially Thomas J. Wertenbaker, *Princeton 1746-1896* (Princeton, 1946), and William H. S. Demarest, *A History of Rutgers College 1766-1924* (New Brunswick, 1924). An earlier history of Princeton was written by President John Maclean, *History of the College of New Jersey* (2 vols.; Philadelphia, 1877), and another by Varnum L. Collins, *Princeton* (New York, 1914). The second volume of Ray Stannard Baker, *Woodrow Wilson Life and Letters* (Garden City, 1927) covers the Wilson years at Princeton in considerable detail and with great sympathy; Arthur S. Link, *Wilson—the Road to the White House* (Princeton, 1947) covers the same ground more briefly and more critically. Nelson R. Burr, *Education in New Jersey 1630-1871* ("Princeton History of New Jersey Series," ed. Thomas J. Wertenbaker [Princeton, 1942]), is a scholarly work and useful for general background. I have also drawn extensively on my own research and publication in the field of American higher education, especially *The Liberal Arts College: A Chapter in American Cultural History* (New Brunswick, 1957).

DEGREE GRANTING COLLEGES AND UNIVERSITIES IN NEW JERSEY
June 1963

Institution and Date Founded	*Degrees Offered*	*Undergraduate Enrollment*
ALMA WHITE COLLEGE Zarephath, New Jersey Arthur K. White, President 1921	B.A. B.S. M.A. M.S.	Full-time 12 men, 5 Women Part-time 16 Men, 17 Women
BLOOMFIELD COLLEGE Bloomfield, New Jersey Theodore A. Rath, President 1926	B.A.	Full-time 499 Men, 122 Women Part-time 255 Men, 44 Women
CALDWELL COLLEGE FOR WOMEN Caldwell, New Jersey Sister M. Marguerite, O. P., President 1939	B.A. B.S. A.A.	Full-time 700 Women Part-time 200 Women
COLLEGE OF SAINT ELIZABETH Convent Station, New Jersey Sister Hildegarde Marie Mahoney, President 1899	B.A. B.S.	Full-time 701 Women Part-time 209 Women
DON BOSCO COLLEGE Newton, New Jersey Very Rev. Aloysius M. Mianchi, S.D.B. President 1928	B.A.	Full-time 94 Men Part-time 5 Men
DREW UNIVERSITY Madison, New Jersey Robert Fisher Oxnam, President 1866	B.A. B.D. M.R.E. S.T.M. M.A. Ph.D.	Full-time 273 Men, 342 Women Part-time 40 Men, 54 Women
FAIRLEIGH DICKINSON UNIVERSITY Rutherford, New Jersey Peter Sammartino, President 1941	B.A. B.S. M.A. D.D.S. M.A. M.S.	Full-time 2937 Men, 1806 Women Part-time 8191 Men, 2039 Women

Graduate Enrollment	Faculty	Affiliation	Control
Part-time 2 Men, 3 Women	14	Pillar of Fire	Board of Trustees 6 members, alumni and denominational representation
Part-time 3 Men	56	United Presbyterian Church	Board of Directors 42 members
	53	Roman Catholic Church	Board of Trustees 13 members
	92	Roman Catholic Church	Board of Trustees [1] 13 members, includes Bishop of the diocese; at least 7 Sisters of Charity of Saint Elizabeth (ex officio, the Mother General and the Assistant Mother), the President of the College, 4 faculty members and 2 lay alumnae.
	14	Roman Catholic Church	Board of Trustees 8 members, mostly alumni
Full-time 135 Men, 21 Women Part-time 197 Men, 62 Women	93	Methodist Church	Board of Trustees 36 members, one-half Methodist clergy
Full-time 1555 Men, 369 Women Part-time	936	Independent	Board of Trustees 5 members

DEGREE GRANTING COLLEGES AND UNIVERSITIES IN NEW JERSEY *(cont.)*
June 1963

Institution and Date Founded	*Degrees Offered*	*Undergraduate Enrollment*
GEORGIAN COURT COLLEGE Lakewood, New Jersey Sister M. Pierre, R.S.M., President 1908	B.A. B.S.	Full-time 380 Women Part-time 2 Men, 71 Women
GLASSBORO STATE COLLEGE Glassboro, New Jersey Thomas E. Robinson, President 1923	B. A. M.A.	Full-time 643 Men, 1388 Women Part-time 556 Men, 1203 Women
IMMACULATE CONCEPTION SEMINARY Darlington, Ramsey P.O., New Jersey Rt. Rev. Monsignor George W. Shea, S.T.D., Rector 1860	B.A. S.T.B.	Full-time 297 Men
JERSEY CITY STATE COLLEGE Jersey City, New Jersey Michael B. Gilligan, President 1927	B.A. M.A.	Full-time 622 Men, 1405 Women Part-time 4 Men, 2 Women
MONMOUTH COLLEGE West Long Branch, New Jersey William G. Van Note, President 1933	B.A. B.S. A.A.	Full-time 1378 Men, 548 Women Part-time 933 Men, 395 Women
MONTCLAIR STATE COLLEGE Upper Montclair, New Jersey E. DeAlton Partridge, President 1908	B.A. M.A.	Full-time 876 Men, 1455 Women
NEWARK COLLEGE OF ENGINEERING Newark, New Jersey Robert W. Van Houten, President 1881	B.S. * M.S. D. Eng. Sc.	Full-time 1986 Men, 21 Women Part-time 1333 Men, 8 Women

* B.S. in Chemical, Civil, Electrical, Industrial and Mechanical Engineering; M.S. in Chemical, Civil, Electrical, Management and Mechanical Engineering; D. Eng.Sc. in Chemical and Electrical Engineering. In addition to degree enrollments 11 certificate programs are offered as well as diverse training programs,

Graduate Enrollment	Faculty	Affiliation	Control
	51	Roman Catholic Church	Board of Trustees 9 members, denominational, lay, and professional representation
	135	State	State Board of Education
Part-time 79 Men, 56 Women			
	27	Roman Catholic Church	Board of Deputies 5 members
	168	State	State Department of Education
Part-time 140			
	128	Independent	Board of Trustees 15 members, including state officials, professionals
Full-time 5 Men, 6 Women Part-time 1064 Men, 327 Women	172	State	State Board of Education
Part-time 878 Men, 7 Women	292	State and Municipal	Board of Trustees 11 members, including ex officio the Governor and the Mayor of Newark, and local business and professional representation

seminars and conferences.

911 students are currently enrolled in individual courses and certificate programs, while 181 are registered for conferences and seminars. Teaching staff, beyond those serving in the undergraduate and graduate faculty totals 125.

DEGREE GRANTING COLLEGES AND UNIVERSITIES IN NEW JERSEY *(cont.)*

June 1963

Institution and Date Founded	*Degrees Offered*	*Undergraduate Enrollment*
NEWARK STATE COLLEGE Union, New Jersey Eugene G. Wilkins, President 1855	B.A. M.A.	Full-time 393 Men, 1499 Women Part-time 1010 Men, 2064 Women
NEW BRUNSWICK THEOLOGICAL SEMINARY New Brunswick, New Jersey Wallace N. Jamison,* President 1784	B.D.	Full-time 52 Men Part-time 5 Men
PATERSON STATE COLLEGE Wayne, New Jersey Marion E. Shea, President 1855	B.A. M.A.	Full-time 411 Men, 1673 Women Part-time 213 Men, 832 Women
PRINCETON THEOLOGICAL SEMINARY Princeton, New Jersey James Iley McCord, President 1812	B.D. M.R.E. Th.M. Th.D.	
PRINCETON UNIVERSITY Princeton, New Jersey Robert Francis Goheen, President 1746	A.B. B.S.E. M.A. M.S.E. M.F.A. M.P.A. Ph.D.	Full-time 3069 Men
RIDER COLLEGE Trenton, New Jersey Franklin F. Moore, President 1865	B.A. B.S. B.S. in Com. B.S. Ed. M.A. A.A.	Full-time 1936 Men, 789 Women

* As of September 1, 1963.

† In addition to the Graduate enrollment listed above, there are 46 (1W) Visiting Fellows and 42 (1 W) Visiting Students, bringing the total graduate enrollment to 102.

Graduate Enrollment	*Faculty*	*Affiliation*	*Control*
	160	State	State Board of Education
Part-time 253 Men, 400 Women			
	16	Reformed Church in America	Board of Superintendents 60 members, denominational representation
	191	State	State Board of Education
Part-time 183 Men, 245 Women			
Full-time 371 Men, 27 Women Part-time 51 Men, 2 Women	44	United Presbyterian Church in the U.S.A.	Board of Trustees 36 members: 18 clergymen, 18 laymen (all members of the United Presbyterian Church in the U.S.A.
Full-time † 932 Men, 9 Women	685	Independent	Board of Trustees 35 members, including the Governor and the President of the University, ex officio, 21 Charter members, 8 alumni, and 4 term members. (Except for the Governor, all members are alumni of Princeton.)
Full-time 3 Men Part-time 38 Men, 23 Women	173	Independent	Board of Trustees 17 members, alumni and professional representation

DEGREE GRANTING COLLEGES AND UNIVERSITIES IN NEW JERSEY *(cont.)*
June 1963

Institution and Date Founded	*Degrees Offered*	*Enrollment Undergraduate*
RUTGERS—THE STATE * UNIVERSITY New Brunswick, New Jersey Mason W. Gross, President 1766	B.A. B.S. A.A. A.S. M.A. M.F.A. M.S. M.B.A. Ed.M. M.L.S. M.S.W. M.C.L. LL.B. Ph.D. Ed.D. Ed. Spec.	Full-time 6468 Men, 3239 Women Part-time 4594 Men, 1641 Women
ST. MICHAEL'S PASSIONIST MONASTERY Union City, New Jersey Very Rev. John C. Ryan, C.P., President and Rector 1866	M.A.	
SAINT PETER'S COLLEGE Jersey City, New Jersey Very Rev. Edward F. Clark, S.J., President 1872	B.A. B.S.	Full-time 1750 Men, 40 Women Part-time 345 Men, 81 Women
SEATON HALL UNIVERSITY † South Orange, New Jersey Most Rev. John J. Dougherty, S.T.L., L.H.D. President 1856	B.A. B.S. B.S. in Bus. Adm. B.S. in Nursing A.A. M.A. M.S. M.B.A. M.D. D.D.S. LL.B. B.S. Ed.	Full-time 2689 Men, 542 Women Part-time 1621 Men, 1406 Women

* All divisions of the University included. Additional locations in Newark, Camden, and Paterson, New Jersey.

† Additional locations in Paterson, Jersey City, and Newark, New Jersey.

Graduate Enrollment	*Faculty*	*Affiliation*	*Control*
Full-time 1149 Men, 236 Women Part-time 2185 Men, 1060 Women	2011	State	Board of Governors 13 members, including the President of the University and the Commissioner of Education ex officio; 6 members appointed by the Governor of the State; 5 elected by and from the Board of Governors
Full-time 19 Men	8	Roman Catholic Church	Board of Trustees 3 members, all clergy
	149	Society of Jesus	Board of Trustees 9 members, denominational representation
Full-time 533 Men, 33 Women Part-time 1702 Men, 533 Women	885	Roman Catholic Archdiocese of Newark	Board of Trustees 15 members

DEGREE GRANTING COLLEGES AND UNIVERSITIES IN NEW JERSEY *(cont.)*
June 1963

Institution and Date Founded	*Degrees Offered*	*Undergraduate Enrollment*
SHELTON COLLEGE Ringwood Borough, New Jersey Arthur E. Steele, President 1908	B.A.	Full-time 63 Men, 61 Women Part-time 26 Men, 22 Women
STEVENS INSTITUTE OF TECHNOLOGY Hoboken, New Jersey Jess H. Davis, President 1870	B.S. B.E. M.S. M.E. Ph.D. Sc.D.	Full-time 1097 Men
TRENTON STATE COLLEGE Trenton, New Jersey President 1855	B.A. M.A.	Full-time 583 Men, 1549 Women Part-time 874 Men, 1263 Women
UPSALA COLLEGE East Orange, New Jersey Evald B. Lawson President 1893	B.A. B.S.	Full-time 839 Men, 664 Women Part-time 374 Men, 232 Women
WESTMINSTER CHOIR COLLEGE Princeton, New Jersey Lee Hastings Bristol, Jr., President 1926	B. Mus. B. Mus. Ed. M. Mus.	Full-time 99 Men, 119 Women Part-time 13 Men, 8 Women

Graduate Enrollment	*Faculty*	*Affiliation*	*Control*
	20	Private	Board of Directors 8 members, professional representation
Full-time 208 Men Part-time 1012	150	Independent	Board of Trustees 29 members, alumni and professional representation
	177	State	State Board of Education
Part-time 257 Men, 115 Women			
	119	Lutheran Church in America	Board of Trustees 18 members, alumni and church representation
Full-time 16 Men, 6 Women Part-time 1 Man, 1 Woman	42	Private	Board of Trustees 33 members, alumni, business men, professional, and denominational representation

INDEX

THE NEW JERSEY HISTORICAL SERIES

Published Under the Auspices of

STATE OF NEW JERSEY TERCENTENARY COMMISSION

PRINTED IN U.S.A.

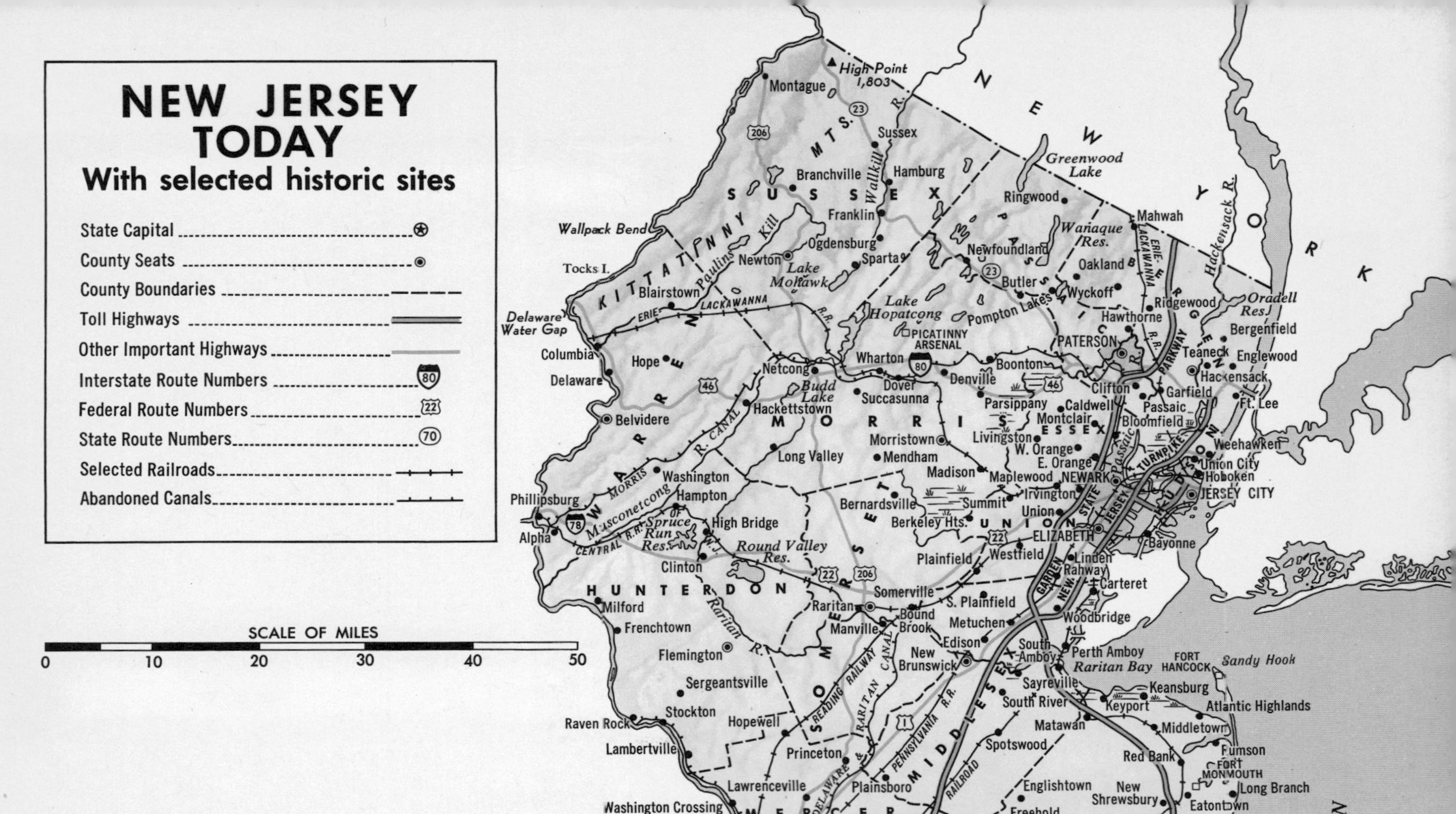
NEW JERSEY TODAY
With selected historic sites
State Capital
County Seats
County Boundaries
Toll Highways
Other Important Highways
Interstate Route Numbers
Federal Route Numbers
State Route Numbers
Selected Railroads
Abandoned Canals
SCALE OF MILES
0 10 20 30 40 50
NEW YORK
SUSSEX
PASSAIC
BERGEN
MORRIS
ESSEX
HUDSON
UNION
WARREN
HUNTERDON
SOMERSET
MIDDLESEX
MERCER
MONMOUTH
KITTATINNY MTS.
High Point 1,803
Montague
Sussex
Branchville
Hamburg
Franklin
Ogdensburg
Sparta
Newton
Lake Mohawk
Wallkill R.
Paulins Kill
Wallpack Bend
Tocks I.
Delaware Water Gap
Blairstown
Columbia
Hope
Delaware
Belvidere
Washington
Hampton
Phillipsburg
Alpha
Musconetcong
Spruce Run Res.
High Bridge
Clinton
Round Valley Res.
Milford
Frenchtown
Flemington
Sergeantsville
Stockton
Raven Rock
Lambertville
Hopewell
Raritan R.
Netcong
Budd Lake
Hackettstown
Long Valley
Mendham
Morristown
Wharton
Dover
Succasunna
Lake Hopatcong
PICATINNY ARSENAL
Denville
Boonton
Parsippany
Livingston
Madison
Bernardsville
Berkeley Hts.
Summit
Greenwood Lake
Ringwood
Wanaque Res.
Newfoundland
Butler
Pompton Lakes
Oakland
Wyckoff
Mahwah
Ridgewood
Hawthorne
PATERSON
Clifton
Passaic
Garfield
Hackensack R.
Oradell Res.
Bergenfield
Teaneck
Englewood
Hackensack
Ft. Lee
Caldwell
Montclair
Bloomfield
W. Orange
E. Orange
Maplewood
NEWARK
Irvington
Union
ELIZABETH
Westfield
Plainfield
Linden
Rahway
Carteret
Weehawken
Union City
Hoboken
JERSEY CITY
Bayonne
Passaic
NEW JERSEY TURNPIKE
GARDEN STATE PARKWAY
Somerville
Raritan
Bound Brook
Manville
S. Plainfield
Metuchen
Edison
Woodbridge
New Brunswick
South Amboy
Perth Amboy
Raritan Bay
Sayreville
South River
FORT HANCOCK
Sandy Hook
Keansburg
Keyport
Atlantic Highlands
Middletown
Matawan
Spotswood
Red Bank
Fumson
FORT MONMOUTH
Long Branch
Eatontown
New Shrewsbury
Englishtown
Freehold
Asbury Park
Princeton
Plainsboro
Hightstown
Lawrenceville
Washington Crossing
West Trenton
TRENTON
ERIE-LACKAWANNA R.R.
MORRIS CANAL
CENTRAL R.R. OF N.J.
READING RAILWAY
RARITAN CANAL
DELAWARE & RARITAN CANAL
PENNSYLVANIA R.R.
PENNSYLVANIA RAILROAD